2020 CONSUMER TREND INSIGHTS

First published in the Republic of Korea in 2020 by Miraebook Publishing Co.

Inquiries should be addressed to
Miraebook Publishing Co.
5th Fl., Miraeui-chang Bldg., 62-1 Jandari-ro, Mapo-ku, Seoul
Tel : 82-2-325-7556 / email : mbookjoa@naver.com

www.miraebook.co(miraebookjoa.blog.me)
Instagram.com/miraebook
Facebook.com/miraebook

ISBN 978 89 5989 644 8 (13320)
CIP CIP2020011072

2020
CONSUMER
TREND
INSIGHTS

Rando Kim · June Young Lee · Miyoung Jeon ·
Hyang Eun Lee · Jihye Choi · Seoyoung Kim · Soojin Lee ·
Youhyun Alex Suh · Jeong Yun Kwon · Dahye Han

Authors

Rando Kim (김난도)

Rando Kim is a professor in the Dept. of Consumer Science(DCS), Seoul National University(SNU) and the head of Consumer Trend Center(CTC), SNU. As a specialist in consumer behavior and market trend analysis, he has written more than 20 books including *Trend Korea series, Trend China, What Consumers Want*, and *Luxury Korea*. He also wrote essay books, *Amor Fati, Future and My Job*, and *Youth, It's Painful* which is sold three million copies in 14 countries. He has conducted research projects about consumer needs finding, new product planning, and market trend probing for Korea's major companies like Samsung, LG, SK, CJ, Hyundai Motors, Amore Pacific, Lotte, Fursys, Nongshim, and Coway.

June Young Lee (이준영)

June Young Lee currently works as an associate professor in Sang-Myung University. He received a doctor's degree in DCS, SNU. He received 'The Best Paper Award' in *The Journal of Consumer Studies*. He worked as a senior researcher in Life Soft Research lab of LG Electronics. He is a laboratory chief of Consumer Research Center in Sang-Myung University.

Miyoung Jeon (전미영)

She currently works as a research fellow in the CTC, SNU. She worked as a research analyst at the Samsung Economic Research Institute. She obtained BA, MA, and PhD degrees in DCS, SNU. She wrote Ph.D. dissertation and subsequent articles about purchasing behavior and consumer happiness. She received 'The Best Publication Award' from the Korean Society of Consumer Studies in 2008. She is interested in tracking consumer trends in Korea and China as well as big data analysis for new product development and industrial application.

Hyang Eun Lee (이향은)

Hyang Eun Lee is an associate professor in the Dept. of Service Design Engineering, Sungshin Women's University. She has a master's degree in Design Management from the Central Saint Martins in London, England and a Ph.D. in Design from the Graduate School of Arts, SNU with dissertation on "A Study on the Process Model Focused on Experience: Centering on Experience of a Designer Transformed into Intuitive Insight." Her main area of research includes UX trends and user psychology, as well as design and consumption trends. She is working at a range of government to corporates in research and developments regarding innovation.

Jihye Choi (최지혜)

Jihye Choi, Ph.D. in Consumer Science from DCS, SNU, works as a research fellow at CTC. She has participated in many consulting projects with Korea's leading companies such as Samsung and LG, and gives public lectures on consumer trends. She currently teaches consumer behavior and qualitative research methodology at SNU. She contributes many articles and columns to major Korean newspapers and media.

Seoyoung Kim (김서영)

Seoyoung Kim completed her Ph.D. course in DCS, SNU and is a founder and CEO of company named "Scandiedu." She received a master's degree in the study of consumption value of married and unmarried women. She coauthored *Trend China* in 2013 through a study of Chinese consumption trends. She is interested in the psychological structure of brain activation status, consumer psychological deviation, and consumer's ambivalence when consumers purchase. Her main research field is the proliferation and prediction of consumer trends in Korea and China

Soojin Lee (이수진)

Soojin Lee has completed BA, MA, and Ph.D. course in DCS, SNU. She has been a senior researcher at CTC since 2015. Prior to joining the center, she was a stock market reporter on Maeil Economic TV. As a contributing researcher, she is conducting a number of consulting projects with clients about consumer trend. She won the first prize in the Korean Academic Society of Financial Planning symposium. Her studies focus on consumer trends, consumption culture, and family economics.

YouHyun Alex Suh (서유현)

YouHyun Alex Suh graduated from Central Saint Martins College of Art & Design Textile BA(Hons) in the UK, London. She achieved an MS degree in Graduate School of Culture Technology, Korea Advanced Institute of Science(KAIST), specialized in design management and consumer behavior. She currently is senior researcher at CTC, and a Ph.D. candidate at SNU, specializing in data-driven trend analysis.

Jeong Yun Kwon (권정윤)

Jeong Yun Kwon is a PhD candidate in DCS, SNU and is currently a senior researcher at CTC. She academically explored the changes in consumers' lives caused by technological change through her master thesis, "Consumer Happiness and Social Comparisons on SNS in Experiential and Material Purchases." Her interests include rapidly changing modern society, its impact on consumer cultures, and various research methodologies to capture them.

Dahye Han (한다혜)

Dahye Han received a BA in the Department of Psychology, SNU and an M.A. degree in DCS, SNU. Currently, she is in the Ph.D. course work in SNU and works as a researcher in CTC. With her masters thesis, "A Study on Consumer Emotion Changes in Online Clothing Purchasing Process," her research interests focus on consumer behavior, trend analysis, and consumption psychology.

Consumer Trend Center, Seoul National University

Consumer Trend Center(CTC) is established in 2004 for the analysis of rapidly changing consumer trends and has announced "ten trend keywords" every year since 2007. CTC has done collaborative researches with many companies, and provided education programs about consumer needs analysis. CTC plans to incorporate into consulting firm named "The Trend Korea Company" which specializes in trend forecasting, generation studies, marketing planning, and new product/service development.

Preface

C hanges are inevitable. "No man ever steps in the same river twice." Greek philosopher Heraclitus' remark lives on from ancient times to this day. Yet now, the speed of its shifts is exponentially accelerated by advancing technologies, the shape of the population, and new communication tools such as internet and social media.

In 2019, Thomas Cook, the worldwide renowned travel company, went broke. Established in 1841, it owned more than 100 airplanes and led the industry by innovations; traveler's cheques, package tours, and exchange services. Over the last 30 years, the travel industry showed rapid growth with an increasing number of travelers each year. But what happened to Thomas Cook? It faced management problems, failed to adapt new traveling patterns, and overlooked the emerging threats of Online Travel Agencies (OTAs).

We live in times where changes happen 'fast and furiously.' In a time like this, 'trend' is becoming more ambiguous yet incredibly crucial. The company's success lies in the hand of the consumer trend. Just as much as knowing the 'right' answer, swiftly responding to the 'trend' will be the key factor in a successful business. It is no more likely to be enough just to offer quality products at a reasonable price. For the first time in human history, enhanced manufacturing capabilities led the balance between supply and demand curves to turn towards a more excessive supply side. This means existing products and services are no longer chosen by customers if they do not fit trends. In short, understanding consumers in and out, and quickly adapting to changing environments of the customers and the market, i.e., trends, is now more than a necessity for survival. Thus, we live in a true "Age of Trends."

Every year since 2008, Trend Korea Company (former 'Consumer Trend Center' at Seoul National University) has published *Trend Korea*, a bestseller book which already became twelve-years-old this year. The readers' attention we get every year is quite incredible but that also proves how the trend is becoming a more crucial factor in our everyday lives. Rooted in a scholastic perspective, we vigorously encourage curiosity towards the culture yet not losing the vivid sense of reality in industries. To do so, we've consulted projects with various industries and major companies including Samsung Electronics, AmorePacific, Hyundai Motors, LG Electronics, CJ E&M, SK Group, etc.

In *Trend Korea*, we announce every year 'The Ten Keywords of Next Year's Trends.' The acronym of keywords is always related to 'the animal of the year', a tradition which East Asia shares. Using the Chinese zodiac animals, we create a word that can symbolize the next year. For example, in the year of the 'horse', the ten keywords formed DARK HORSES; for the year of the rooster, it was

CHICKEN RUN. For 2020, the year of the rat, the acronym for the keywords forms MIGHTY MICE. Mighty Mouse, a superhero cartoon character created in the 1940s, reflects the recent trends of 'Newtro'(New+Retro, meaning 'revialism') and captures the movement of needs for the small but strong superheroes in recent economic crises and pandemic of corona virus.

As suggested at the title, the keywords in *Trend Korea* were primarily targeted for Korean circumstances, but as the years go on, we found most of them are universally applicable. This 'glocal' phenomenon is powered by the internet and social media which converge trends all over the world and spread it at the same time. However, when scrutinizing trends, we do not only look at our own country. Two more possible reasons for its international resemblance are that our research team considers data worldwide — U.S., Europe, Japan, and China — from the beginning, and that the Korean market is often working as a "test bed" for global market standards.

For years, I have been asked by English-speaking executives of multinational companies in Korea and foreign journalists to translate *Trend Korea* into English. Over the years, I also came to believe the possibility of the keywords in the book could help designers, developers, marketers, and managers working in many countries with a global market to better understand the changes in their customers and the market. Thus, I decide to have this book translated into English, starting this year. Instead of being translated word-for-word, the English translation has tried to include content more universally applicable to the various markets in the world by modifying and complementing the original content.

It gives me a great pleasure to acknowledge for the help of making this book. First of all, I am grateful to the voluntary trend hunters of CTC, 'Trenders Nal' for their collection of useful trend artifacts, which emerge into ten keywords in the book. I particularly want to thank Guihwa H. Blanz, Seung Kyung Kim, and YouHyun Alex Suh for the efforts of translation. The translation process was a tough challenge because the original book, *Trend Korea 2020*, was written by many newly-coined words in the context of Korean language and cultural settings. They have done liberal translations perfectly within short time in spite of many difficulties. I also express my special thank to CEO Eui Hyun Sung and staff members of Miraebook Publishing Co., who encouraged me to publish English version of the book. Lastly, I have to thank my co-authors who generated great ideas and first drafts of trend keywords. This book may not be possible without their talents and dedications.

As it always has been, it's hard to foresee what will happen in the world economy of 2020. The market is full of uncertainty, but I hope the keywords in this book may be used as a compass, a guide, to accompany you through the volatile changes in consumer behavior.

Rando Kim
Professor, Department of Consumer Science,
Seoul National University
CEO, Trend Korea Company

CONTENTS

MIGHTY MICE

10 trend keywords
of 'the Year of Mouse'

Me and Myselves
Multi-persona

Today, people have multiple identities which are divided in many ways. Multiple identities are created in various situations with different social media channels that we use on daily bases. This multi-layered self-image — as we call "multi-personas" — is like having multiple masks in day-to-day life. The concept of multi-persona is a key concept that helps us understand the underlying cause of contemporary consumption trends — such as ambivalent consumer behaviors, pursuit of taste-based identity, gender-free trends, and digital mythomania — not to mention other subsequent keywords addressed in this book.

Immediate Satisfaction:
the 'Last Fit Economy'

The last-minute experiences became the critical factor of consumers' choice. I coined the term "last fit economy" for optimizing customer satisfaction of short distance economy in the last moment of acquiring goods. The last fit economy includes (1) 'the last fit of delivery,' which is about eliminating the hassle of shopping by providing convenient delivery up to the last point of contact with customers; (2) 'the last fit of mobility,' which is about helping people reach their target destination as conveniently as possible; and (3) 'the last fit of purchasing journey', which is about providing a satisfying grand finale to all purchasing journeys and experiences. Businesses have to move one step ahead beyond the product-centered differentiation, and they have to pay more attention to the very intimate moment when they make contact with customers. Those who seize that last minute will seize the market.

Goodness and Fairness:
Fair Player

The pursuit of goodness and fairness will become stronger. Employees expect to have their contributions fairly recognized even if they are at the bottom of the corporate ladder. Domestic chores must be divided equally among all family members. Students prefer individual assignments over team projects and tests with multiple-choice questions over writing essays on the questions. When making purchases, consumers care about the "good influence" of a brand as well as products themselves. The younger generation, who have grown up in a society where individuality has become an important value, expresses their desire for fairness, goodness and effectiveness through various media and consumption behaviors. The generation that is pursuing fairness more than any other generation is coming into their own. It is urgent for companies to make major directional changes in their organizational management and CSR activities.

Here and Now:
the 'Streaming Life'

Not just in the way people listen to music, but the way of life itself is changing from downloading to streaming. Streaming technology plays audio or video through a network, and it has the advantage of allowing people to experience content without having to download and own it. In addition to music or movie, people today prefer a method where they experience — space or products — with options in a very short period of time as if they were streaming while moving around. The way of life chosen by the younger generation — with their inflated desires but limited resources — is a nomadic lifestyle that focuses on experience rather than possession. To cater to the needs of these experience-gathering consumers, businesses need to focus not on increasing the number of buyers, but paying attention to the segmentation within consumers and managing their entire streaming journey.

Technology of Hyper-Personalization
Data-driven personalization

What would be the destination of the remarkably advancing latest cutting-edge technologies, such as artificial intelligence, big data, object recognition, 5G? In the end, it will be about "please suit my needs, and do it so differently by exactly comprehending my intimate personal situations." Now, the market segmentation operates on a unit of 0.1 consumers. A technology that understands each consumer's situation and the context in real-time will predict their needs, provide services and products accordingly. We state this stage of technology as "hyper-personalization." This technology allows each consumer to have their most wanted experience at the right moment by segmenting each consumers' situation. The technology nowadays has progressed to the point where it can figure out what customers want based on their consumption patterns and it can preemptively provide what they want. The industry's challenge will be in the hands of how we fragmentize a customer's preferences into thousands of suggestions and yet precisely mold it into one person.

You're with Us,
'Fansumer'

Consumers are not easily satisfied by simply purchasing one option. They now have a desire to personally participate and invest in the manufacturing process of developing products, brands, and stars. This new type of consumer who takes part in the entire life cycle of a product and exercising their control over it is termed a "fansumer." They actively support and purchase a product with the pride of 'having raised it personally.' The fansumers' influence is continuously expanding, and it includes participating in crowd-funding, engaging in supporter activities, rooting for or criticizing celebrities and influencers, and many more. Now, just being "with the customers" is not enough. In the market of fansumers guided "by the customers," businesses have to first reach out to their consumers to get their enthusiastic support and participation.

Make or Break, Specialize or Die
Specialization

You have to specialize to survive. Assured satisfaction of a
selected few has become more important than appealing to
all customers. As the development of online distribution has
activated a long-tail economy, the overheated competition
has made it difficult to notice differences between products.
As consumer needs have grown extremely individualized,
the standardized mass-market approach will not help
businesses gain consumers. Specialization is more than just
a point of differentiation; it is now a condition for survival.
Sort out customer characteristics like tweezers, zoom in
on customer needs like a microscope, compartmentalize
commercial zones like a compass, and focus on the
company's competitiveness like a fishing rod. Now, the niche
becomes the rich.

Iridescent Opal:
the New 5060 Generation

A new group of consumers called the "OPAL generation" is emerging. OPAL stands for "Old People with Active Lives." The term also embraces the idea that the colorful characteristics these people display resemble the opal gemstone, which is said to contain the colors of all gemstones. This new middle-aged group of consumers born in the 1950s and 1960s, which includes baby boomers, is rising to the challenge of working in new jobs, enjoying dynamic leisure activities and purchasing their own content products, consequently bringing the winds of change to various industries. The OPAL generation, who vigorously uses YouTube and new technologies as freely as younger people, is playing a key role in society and will provide fresh energy to the stagnant market.

Convenium:
Convenience as a Premium

Convenience is premium. As the standard of purchase is shifting from cost-effectiveness to premiums, the new standard of premiums for modern consumers — who have many things they want to do but not enough time to do them all — is anything that saves them time and effort. People today value experience but they are always short of time. These days, even their personal ties to communities where they used to reach out to ask for a small favor have been growing weaker. In the meantime, the shortage of available jobs has given rise to the number of "bridge workers" who are willing to provide their labor at any time. With the development of the "app economy" that connects this supply to its demand, convenium is becoming an essential trend. People say we are in a bad recession, but where customers experience small inconveniences, there exist opportunities.

Elevate Yourself:
Birth of Self-upgraders

Upgrade yourself! A new group of people who pursues growth rather than success has emerged: Self-upgraders. Their priority is making "today's me better than yesterday's me" by managing their life's career instead of managing simple qualifications to win competition against others. The self-upgrading trend is the result of the changing paradigm of life and career management, as the 52-hour workweek system is implemented, the concept of lifetime employment is disappearing, and the population is rapidly aging. The rise of the self-upgraders who desire qualitative change in their life is turning experience economy into "transformation economy." The happiness of consumers is moving towards the point of balance between meaningfulness and the fun of self-growth.

Me and Myselves

Multi-persona

The word "myself" might as well become "myselves," as people today possess various multiple identities. An identity assumed at work is different from an at-home identity; a general day-to-day identity is different from a fandom identity; and offline identity is different from a social media identity. Even on social media, people assume different identities depending on whether they are on YouTube, Twitter, or Instagram. Even within the same social media platform, people create multiple accounts, switching their identities from one account to another. Like a Chinese Bian Lian performer who changes his masks from one to another almost instantaneously, consumers today change into different individuals from moment to moment. Academically, these masks are called "personas."

The word "persona" originally referred to a theatrical mask used in ancient Greece. Today, it is used in psychology to refer to one's external personality projected onto others. As society is gradually changing to accommodate complex and individualized multimedia, the persona is emerging as an important concept. Recent trends of various types and patterns can be viewed as a result of "people changing their masks depending on their situations." I would like to call these different masks "multi-personas."

While multi-personas have expanded the possibilities of human pluralism, paradoxically, the foundation of people's identity has become very unstable. Society needs to watch out for the side effect of technology overdetermining consumer identity. Companies need to make an effort to engage in flexible communication appropriate for customers' diversified identities and circumstances. What does it mean to "be myself"? Who is the real me? Multimedia society presents tough questions.

People today are good at "mode switching." Who people are at work is different from who they are once they return home. Who people are at home is different from who they are outside. Who people are on an ordinary day is different from who they are while traveling. It is also not unusual to find an otherwise soft-spoken person turn into a passionate warrior when talking politics, and an ordinary housewife to turn into an "ARMY" with her sparkling eyes when talking about BTS.

One of the biggest tendencies exhibited by current trends is that the distinction between the "real me" and the "different me" becomes clearer, and consuming behavior that fits the identity of the situation becomes more important because different consuming contexts end up segmenting the identity of each consumer according to that context. Given that millennials are good at mode switching and that their way of life is becoming more segmented depending on the multiplicity of situations they find themselves in, what does it mean that the "real me" is becoming multifaceted? What would be the common root cause underlying these trends? If we can understand that cause, we will be able to understand — on a more fundamental level — the current changes in trends that are complex and appear to conflict with each other. What could be the most important underlying cause for all these changes?

The answer may be found in the fact that people today possess identities that can be variously differentiated. An identity assumed at work is different from an at-home identity; a general day-to-day identity is different from a fandom identity; and an offline identity is different from a social media identity. Even on social media, people assume different identities depending on whether they are on YouTube, Twitter, or Instagram. The thing is that people do not find it awkward splitting their identities at all. This is a big change.

In the past, those who have split identities like "Jekyll and Hyde" were considered to have dissociative identity disorder. That is, they were considered to have a sort of mental illness. In today's world, however, the separation of identity has become natural and necessary just as a Chinese Bian Lian performer needs to change his masks from moment to moment. Academically, these masks are called "personas."

> "Humans have a thousand personas, and they make relationships wearing an appropriate persona according to situation."
>
> – Carl Gustav Jung

Persona is a term used in psychology to refer to one's external personality projected onto others. The word persona originally referred to a theatrical mask used in ancient Greece. Carl Jung imported the term to psychology and explained that people have a thousand personas and wear an appropriate persona according to a given situation.

Persona is not a new term, but as society is changing to accommodate complex and individualized multimedia, persona is emerging as an important concept. In other words, the underlying cause that cuts through many recent trends can be seen as a result of "people changing their masks depending on their situations." These multiple masks could be called "multi-personas."

The Concept and Background of Persona

Persona is actually a difficult concept, but in recent years it has become more familiar. One of the reasons may be that in their new album, BTS, the global boy band, asked the question "Who am I?" and made the question of identity, that is, persona, a global topic. In fact, "Who am I?" is a very fundamental question commonly found in myths of many cultures. Perhaps all religions exist to find answers to this question. Humans have always experienced an identity crisis, but the crisis is intensifying in modern times. Let's look into some background to understand why.

Multiple Identities in Nomadic Society

A person's identity was traditionally formed based on lineage and occupation. The family name that each of us has is a product of paternity, and in the past, people often took their names from their occupations. Lineage and occupation were very stable foundations. However, modern-day people are distinguished by increased nomadism; that is, people move instead of settle. As society is creating a more fractionated individual, lineage is becoming less important. As for occupation, people now keep multiple jobs in a so-called gig economy, performing multiple tasks. As a result, the foundation of identity is dissolving. The time of the "flexible self" is upon us.

The manifestation of various identities takes place in the form of multi-personas, instead of uniformly belonging to a single self. These multi-personas transcend time and space; they are continuously updated; they constantly change through interactions; and they are capable of quick "mode switching" to a completely different form because they can be reset. In other words, identity is changing into a relative, fluid concept, instead of an absolute, never-changing one. In particular, the "identity play" on the internet is not about reproducing reality as it is. That is, people engaging in "identity play" enjoy a broader degree of freedom through imagination, fusion, and transformation.

Trans-Identity in Online Space

Identities can change in a much wider range than before. This is made possible because various combinations of identities are now possible due to the development of many online platforms. While offline identities based on lineage or occupation grow less significant, a festival of all sorts of diverse personas is happening on the online stage.

For example, online game users often lie about their age. They do this either to establish a hierarchy based on age or to pretend they belong to the right age group. When choosing a game character, some people pick a different gender than their own. So, they become trans-gender in the game.

For virtual identities, defining a self in terms of social roles or lineage is not important. Virtual identities have a so-called disembodied characteristic, which has nothing to do with actual gender, age, and social class. Furthermore, virtual identities keep being re-configured into different characters that can have all sorts of combinations that defy existing patterns. In this way, "myself" is evolving into plural "myselves," or multiple identities.

This phenomenon is called trans-identity. As indicated by the prefix, trans-identity means the ability to come in and out of multiple identities. Superheroes such as Batman, the Hulk, and Superman are characters with multiple identities. In the online space, ordinary people can also become heroes while moving in and out of reality and virtual reality.[1]

Multi-Accounts in Social Media

On social media platforms, people not only manage their main account but a growing number of "side accounts" featuring their various interests in, for example, exercise, food, pets, and studying. Some side accounts are "specialized accounts" where people post everything about their favorite celebrity or every note from their study sessions. Other side accounts are "taste accounts" where people keep a collection of their doodling, pictures of an injury, or pictures of statues in a city. People used to post their diverse daily activities and interests on one social media account, like displaying products in a department store. Now, however, people are creating various accounts on different social media channels to compartmentalize their posts according to their interests. These accounts, through hashtags, enable people to connect and communicate with others.

Every time people move from one account to another, they assume a different role as if they were actors changing

Creating multiple online accounts with different identities is a global phenomenon. Each Internet user today is reportedly have an average of 7.6 accounts.

masks on a stage. This phenomenon has been intensified as social media services have become more diverse, and specialized or taste-based accounts are on the rise. People used to post all of their interests and daily activities on a single "hot" social media service. If another service became hotter, they would start using that platform and post all of their posts there. But now, there is no longer one dominant social network service. People tend to use different services with different purposes. For example, Facebook may be more for writing text or managing existing relationships, Instagram for posting images, and Twitter for communicating political statements. Each account assumes a different persona, and one's diverse identities can be maintained this way. People used to criticize those who post too often. Now, people admire those who excel at posting daily activities in an interesting and attractive way. This makes side accounts more important.

Creating multiple online accounts with different identities is a global phenomenon. According to a Global WebIndex, more than 98 percent of Internet users use social media, and each user has an average of 7.6 accounts. In fact, Generation Z users have two or more Instagram accounts, and they project antithetical lifestyles and identities on each account.[2] For example, one account can be what they call a Rinsta (real Instagram) and the other can be a Finsta (fake Instagram). They use Rinsta to show a sophisticated and ideal self, and Finsta to show an authentic and natural self. Paradoxically, Rinsta expresses exaggeration and fakeness while Finsta expresses truth and reality.

Social Networking Services for Privacy

There is another type of account — anonymous accounts. More intimate than side accounts, anonymous accounts are used to confide secrets, share strange interests others may find difficult to understand, or talk about sexual desires and fantasies. Therefore, people tend to be more honest and candid about themselves on anonymous accounts, and visitors tend be more interested and sympathetic. Social media platforms where people share their stories anonymously with diverse groups of people are increasing. People use these platforms to express their honest thoughts and identities. Alternatively, people also open accounts that they share only with a few close friends when they become tired of all the connections on social media. This is a contradictory situation where they are creating a type of minimalism in their network of relationships via side accounts.[3]

Increasing anonymous accounts and sites implies that social networking platforms are shifting from a place for connecting with others to a place for freely expressing themselves and creating identities. Facebook CEO Mark Zuckerberg said in March 2019 that "Facebook and Instagram have helped people connect with friends, communities, and interests in the digital equivalent of a town square. But people increasingly also want to connect privately in the digital equivalent of the living room." And he stressed that in the future, "a privacy-focused communications platform will become even more important than today's open platforms." All this points to a growing alertness about open social media where personal information is exposed to unspecified groups of people and where words, once posted, can never be forgotten.

There is a growing demand for digital space where people

Consumers today change into different people
from moment to moment.
What does it mean to "be myself"?
Who is the real me?

can build and create their own lives more comfortably. In sum, social network platforms as a networking tool are becoming less important, while their role as a private space that people enjoy is becoming more important. Social network platforms are becoming a place where people can freely express and realize their identities.[4]

Identity in Selfies

A selling point of the latest smartphones is their excellent cameras. One of the most important and desired features of a smartphone is that it takes a great photo, especially, a selfie. In a common scene, people raise their smartphone to take a picture of themselves. Selfies have become a regular part of our life and have contributed to the spread of the multi-persona syndrome.

In her book, *Je Selfie Donc Je suis* (I Selfie Therefore I Am), Elsa Godart refers to the current times as the "selfie stage" where humans build new relationships with self and the world through digital technology. Philosopher Jacques Lacan referred to the period when infants recognize themselves in a mirror for the first time and start building relationships with others as the "mirror stage." Applying Lacan's theory to us, the screen of a smartphone is a mirror, and our virtual selves meet others through the screen. The selfie stage has much in common with the mirror stage.[5]

In the selfie stage, people can no longer understand

who they are without their virtual self in photos, because people prefer to remain as images reproduced through selfies rather than real-life selves. These days, people don't just take selfies: they use various filters and apps to edit and modify their images. In the past, all the photos of a person looked similar; nowadays, selfies represent "pluralized selves." It is because people care a lot about how they are presented to and perceived by others. As a result, many selves on cyberspace, including social media services, are different from each other, and the difference between selves in reality and selves in cyberspace also grows larger. Problems of self-discrepancy, self-estrangement, and self-split are coming to the fore.[6]

It has also been suggested that identity splitting is a result of a pluralized society. In his book, *Myself and the Others*, Austrian philosopher Isolde Karim defines the present era as the age of pluralization. According to Karim, people in modern society live with "others" who have different identities in terms of their nationality, race, skin color, cultural sensitivity, and sexual orientation. With destroyed homogeneity, people are endlessly engaged in self-reconstruction depending on who they are around and how their situations change. People are living in an era of "metuation (me+situation)." Under this circumstance, natural identity no longer exists.

Pluralization has become an irreversible process and

characteristic of modern society. In a society with advanced pluralization, people constantly ask, "Who should I think I am?" The question of "Who am I?" is already difficult enough, but now, we also need to ask ourselves how we should think about us.[7]

Many Forms of Multi-personas

How is the multi-persona phenomenon manifested in the market? Let us take a brief look into five cases that have direct relevance: (1) increase in ambivalent consumer behavior, (2) development of communities of taste, (3) craze for character products and merchandise, (4) flexible gender expression in the fashion and beauty industries, and (5) digital mythomania and loose personal ties in digital space.

1. Increase in Ambivalent Consumer Behavior

"Going forward, only super-cheap products and premium products will survive," Chung Yong-jin, the vice chairman of Shinsegae Group, allegedly said.[8] Shinsegae operates both super-cheap "No Brand Burger" and high-priced premium "Johnny Rocket Burger" restaurants. Actually, this kind of polarized consumption has been going on for quite some time now. The important question is why. In the past, we thought that wealthy consumers purchased premium products, and poor consumers purchased super-cheap products. These days, however, a single consumer buys both cheap and expensive burgers. For example, people will buy a cheap burger when they just need to eat something for a meal, but they will buy an expensive premium burger when they are on a nice date. The term "ambivalent" consumption seems more accurate than "polarized" consumption. It is also called "Janus consumption," alluding to Janus, the two-faced god from Roman mythology.

Janus consumption exists in the market under many forms. Buying expensive luxury goods for a few items they care about the most while buying super-cheap goods for all the other items is an example of ambivalent Janus consumption. The fact that "cost-effectiveness" and "premium" can be on the same playing field also reflects this ambivalence. This ambivalent consumption can be easily understood with multi-personas: Consumers wear a different mask depending on the situation, and the characteristics of the persona determine the choice between cost-effectiveness and premium.

2. Taste: A Tool for Identity Manifestation

Taste in modern society is more than just hobbies people personally enjoy. In order to satisfy their desire for communication and a sense of belonging, people make connections on social networking platforms based on shared tastes. People also strengthen their identities by continuously sharing and enjoying their tastes together. The emphasis on taste is also closely related to the aforementioned changes in occupation-based identity. There were times when people were named after their occupations. Nowadays, however, job-based identities are only temporary because it is uncertain how many years one will hold on to the same job. In a society where people start dreaming of finding a new job as soon as they get hired, millennials find taste-based identities, focused on achieving "small but certain happiness," more important than occupation-based identities.

Those who turn their hobbies into occupations are also growing in number. Being called a "maniac" used to have a negative connotation, but now maniacs are respected as people who can make money with their hobbies. This trend has given birth to a few newly coined terms, such as "hobbypreneur", which means a business grown out of hobbies, and hoccupation, which combines hobby and occupation.

As taste becomes more important, "What is my real taste?" becomes a crucial question as well. This is why one-day classes where people can try out different new hobbies, one on each day, are becoming popular. "What do I really like?" is an important question we all need to answer.

3. Craze for Character Products and Merchandise

As taste identity becomes more important, more people are

expressing their multi-faceted identities through consumption. One good example is making oneself into a character. The Samsung Galaxy S10 and Galaxy Note 10, released in 2019, have enhanced memojis (emojis based on oneself as a character) by providing a feature where people can create a virtual character in augmented reality and that character mimics the movements that they make in the external world. iPhones also introduced a new feature in iOS 13 that enables users to show their own memojis to others when exchanging texts messages. In a way, these memoji characters in smartphones are part of one's set of multi-personas, which is similar to but different from the real self.

Merchandise is also evolving to accommodate the ability to "express oneself." In Korea until 2014, merchandise was based on fandom culture for idols, celebrities, animation, etc. Since 2015, however, the meanings and targets of merchandise have expanded as merchandise has started to express political and social identities. In fact, traditional merchandise based on idols, celebrities, and animations is on the decline, while merchandise with which people can express and share their values and identities is on the rise. It is notable that characters from messenger apps like KakaoTalk (Korea's most popular messenger app similar to WhatsApp) are becoming hugely popular in real life. People use merchandise and characters to express themselves and feel a sense of belonging and solidarity.

According to a big data analysis conducted by HS Ad, one of the greatest needs consumers satisfy through merchandise is "desire to possess." This suggests that merchandise functions as expanded selves. That is, people expand their identity through acquisition of merchandise. At the center of the craze for characters, therefore, lies more than the satisfaction people get from cute and pretty items. Therein lies people's desire to express their identities. In a way, characters are avatars that express people's identities.

4. Gender-free Trends

The theme of Gucci's fashion show for 2019 F/W collection was "persona." The show wanted to communicate human ambiguity; that is, people become totally different people depending on whether they wear a mask or not. The models in the show were presented in a way that was ambiguous about whether they were men or women. Even their faces were made hard to recognize. Being true to the theme of persona, the models were wearing red masks or masks with studs that fully covered their faces. Before the show, Gucci had also sent out as an invitation the masks of Hermaphroditus from Greek mythology. As a son of Hermes and Aphrodite, Hermaphroditus represents androgyny. He became the symbol for the Gucci collection. Not only for Gucci, but for many fashion brands, one of the most important recent trends is gender neutrality.

While existing unisex fashion has focused on "suiting both men and women well," gender neutrality focuses on gender identities that change freely depending on people's taste without being restricted to their actual gender. It allows both men and women to express and showcase their diverse personas as they please. Good examples include the increasing number of "men who wear makeup" and the emergence of the "corset-free movement" where women break free from restrictive uniform standards of beauty.

5. Digital Mythomania and Loose Personal Ties

Vlogs, videos featuring daily activities using a video sharing site like YouTube, are gaining popularity. Unlike video channels specializing in food, beauty, or games, vlogs do not specialize in a certain topic or information. Vloggers do not have to be talented or professional like specialized YouTubers. Some vlogs are created by office workers sharing their daily activities at work, others are created by stay-at-home mothers sharing their daily childcare, and others are created by students or people who are preparing for national exams sharing their daily studying.

"Get Ready With Me (GRWM)" is a type of vlog that shows people getting ready to go to work in the morning. It is so popular that Google Korea chose GRWM as a keyword for YouTube of 2019. One GRWM clip, "Get Ready to Go To School with Me, a Law Student" by a YouTuber named Tweety was so popular that it recorded over 2.37 million views. Vlogs created by ordinary people are gaining popularity because people can feel a certain connection and a sense of unity. By watching vloggers' ordinary daily lives, people feel that the vloggers' lives are not much different from theirs.[9]

In the online environment, people have more freedom and control over how to show and direct themselves. In doing so, people more easily manage impressions other people make of them because they can freely display their ideal selves, which are different from their real-life offline selves. These vlogs do not just show how things are "as is," however. Vloggers pick and edit scenes so that only the scenes that they want other to see are shown, and they display a version of themselves that is different from the real self. This can be viewed as a kind of digital mythomania. One of the symptoms of mythomania is that people who tell lies come to actually believe those lies. Similarly, people who wear multi-persona masks on vlogs or social media often come to eventually believe that those masks are their real selves.

In guest houses young people often use when traveling alone, guests often get together in the evening to have a small party with drinks and music. They are total strangers from all over the place, but they often share their personal intimate stories surprisingly candidly with each other. This is because they think they are unlikely to see each other ever again. This can be called "the guest house party effect."[10] People can be more honest and candid than usual when they are protected by anonymity or loose ties. The recent trend among millennials joining "loosely tied offline social groups" such as running clubs, salons, and social dining events can be similarly explained.

Studies show that the average number of friends people have in their offline environment is just around 10 while the average number of Facebook friends is around 250. It suggests that people rarely know all their Facebook friends that well. This is why social media users experience the guest house party effect in a paradoxical way in that they can express their ideal selves more freely to those friends they do not really know that well.

Implications

In the future, AI and big data analyses will be able to create multi-personas artificially. Instead of people discovering tastes and hobbies by themselves, AI algorithms will analyze their tastes and curate their identities. Actually, this is already being implemented through a variety of hyper-personalized customized content services. For example, Netflix introduced a technology that identifies consumers' tastes and suggests films that fit their tastes the most on the first page by carefully analyzing data on directors, genres, story development patterns, main characters, etc. The number of Netflix's movie genres in current use is a staggering 70,000 and counting.

Such curation is not just a matter of convenience. It may look like consumers are freely choosing content based on their own tastes, but the truth is, tastes are collected and formed artificially by machines. Consequently, people's tastes can be biased by machines, and existing biases can be intensified. Will it be possible to cultivate active and self-developing tastes and personas? For example, what if a consumer who likes hip-hop music listened to new age music while studying for exams, and the machine kept suggesting new age music later on? People might face a situation where they are forced into specific tastes based on a few choices they have made, even though those are not what they really like. The risk is that this kind of situation is quite likely to be abused and misused politically and commercially.

What implications does the multi-persona trend have for businesses? First, businesses need to change their communication methods. As mentioned previously, people today have multi-personas across multiple social media channels. Therefore, businesses need to come up with individual strategies based on the characteristics of different social media platforms. Businesses need to understand characteristics of social media platforms and analyze which identities people display on each platform. As social media channels are becoming more volatile and spontaneous, more intuitive and sense-centered approaches are needed. It is also useful to approach identity creation not too seriously as if it is a game to play. Soft and comfortable approaches like vlogs that provide gentle solace and sympathy may prove useful.

As for consumers, they will need to learn to accept their "virtual self" and the "real self" in a connected way. In the virtual online space, people need to be wary of disparaging others, committing inhumane deviant behaviors, or showing off by spending conspicuously. People need to earnestly contemplate how to build true relationships in the virtual world. They also need to use online space as a plaza where they can manifest their responsible and free selves.

While multi-personas have expanded the possibilities of human pluralism, paradoxically, the foundation of people's identity has become very unstable. In an era of individualism where people have to constantly define themselves, a key task becomes how to enable atomized individuals to form solid identities. What does it mean to "be myself"? Who is the real me? Multimedia society presents tough questions.

Immediate Satisfaction

the 'Last Fit Economy'

Experiences occurring at the last minute have become critical. The expression "the last mile" originally referred to the distance between death row and to the death chamber, but these days, it is widely used in the distribution industry to mean the final leg in the supply chain where products are delivered to customers. Lately, noticeable efforts have been made in various industries to improve customer satisfaction at this last point of contact, not to mention the last mile in the logistics industry. I term the short distance economy of optimizing customer satisfaction in the last moment "the last fit economy." The last fit economy includes (1) 'the last fit of delivery,' which is about eliminating the hassle of shopping by providing convenient delivery up to the last point of contact with customers; (2) 'the last fit of mobility,' which is about helping people reach their target destination as conveniently as possible; and (3) 'the last fit of purchasing journey,' which is about providing a satisfying grand finale to all purchasing journeys and experiences.

Customers now make their purchase decisions based more on subjective utility than on product features or brand values. Furthermore, the last fit economy is becoming an important factor that changes market dynamics as the number of single-person households is increasing and as millennials and Generation Z, for whom subjective tastes and satisfaction are critical, become the driving force in the market. The era of cost-effectiveness and product features is receding into the past, and now the quality of services is changing customer satisfaction. In this new economy, customer satisfaction at the point of contact where products meet customers is more important than product performance itself. Businesses have to move one step beyond the product-centered repetitive imitation and differentiation competition, and they have to pay more attention to the intimate moment when they make contact with customers. Those who seize that last minute will seize the market.

Suppose you need to buy a pound of beef. What factors would you consider? You would compare the price, grade, quality, origin, and brand of different options. These product details are called "key buying factors" — the important criteria that consumers consider when making a purchase decision. Recently, however, a new key buying factor has emerged: "How fresh, fast, and accurately can you deliver?" Of course, the fundamental reason behind this new factor is the growing importance of delivery in the wake of increasing "untact(meaning "contactless")" orders people make over a cell phone and online. But what calls for our attention is the fact that the customer priorities are changing with regards to these key buying factors.

The standards that guide purchase decisions are also changing. Today's consumers care more about their satisfaction than the price itself when purchasing a product. Therefore, consumers are more than willing to pay money for the products that provide them with immediate satisfaction even when the products are a bit pricey. Now, consumers make purchase decisions based on the product's subjective utility that they can appreciate the moment the product enters their lives, rather than on objective factors like the brand value or the features of the product. In other words, the standards that determine whether a product can satisfy the customer or not is the last point where a product comes into direct contact with the consumer. Emphasizing the importance of customer satisfaction at the last point of contact with customers, we can call this purchasing paradigm change, the "Last Fit Economy." This indicates "a short distance economy that instantaneously optimizes customer satisfaction at the last moment of purchase."

The emergence of the last fit economy suggests that price comparison is no longer the primary strategy in purchase decisions. Consumers are now reluctant to go through a complex decision-making process. Once they recognize the need for a product, their subsequent action leads to "buy it now." To the consumers, the convenience of signing up for paid membership and clicking a button to have their orders delivered to the door the very next morning is more attractive than the inconvenience of having to personally go out and find where to buy the same price at a cheaper price. This trend means the consumers' decision-making criteria are shifting from utility-per-price to utility-per-effort. Perhaps for this reason, the cost-effectiveness principle is now working in fewer and fewer domains even in the long-term recession. The main reason behind this is the consumers' decision-making criteria that are shifting from the utility of a product to the quality of service. It means that for consumers, their optimized satisfaction at the last minute of the buying process has become more important.

"Last Fit" is a term inspired by the word "last mile." Last mile was used in the past to indicate the distance a death row inmate walked to the execution chamber, but today, it is widely used in the telecommunication industry to refer to the last mile in the process of connecting network cables to each household. This term has spread to the logistics industry to indicate "the last leg in the process of delivering a product to the customer," because this last mile determines the quality of service and also influences the ultimate level of consumer satisfaction.

Following the latest development in home delivery logistics, the last mile where the product is delivered to the door of the customer, or the delivery itself, is emerging as an important issue, but in the last fit economy, delivery is only a partial concept. There are three types of last fit: (1) The last fit in delivery that eliminates the hassle of shopping by providing convenient delivery service to the last point of contact with customers; (2) The last fit in mobility that helps customers access their destination most comfortably; and (3) The last fit in the purchasing journey that adds satisfying perks to the end of all journeys, be it of a purchase or a user experience.

Various Forms of the Last Fit Economy

1. Last Fit in Delivery

Currently, a hot topic in the domestic delivery industry is "dawn." The distribution businesses are in a life and death competition over who can reach the consumers' doors fastest. As if early morning delivery is not fast enough, some distribution businesses are tapping into the faster "midnight delivery."

While Market Kurly마켓컬리, an online grocery startup, is the leader in early morning delivery and boasts a significant market share, other traditional distribution leaders such as Shinsegae신세계 and Lotte롯데 have also jumped into early morning delivery services, and the home shopping industry is also joining in this fierce race. A new logistics service that allows consumers to receive their orders at 4 a.m. if ordered the previous evening is heralding the dawn in Korea.

These businesses offer more than just fast delivery. They also attract consumers by overhauling their selection of products. For example, they launch special categories such as those which are exclusive for vegan customers or vegetarians, or offer produce items that are fresher and cheaper by reducing supply chain and distribution margins.

This trend is expanding to other industries as well. In fact, new ways to improve delivery systems are emerging across all industries. One good example is the furniture industry, which used to be considered a traditional offline industry, but now, even the furniture industry is launching an all-out campaign with "next day delivery service." In the past, it took four days and up to a week for a furniture order to be delivered to the customer, but now, they reduced the delivery and even installation time to just one day, and realized a next-day delivery service so that customers can receive the order quickly as long as they place it before 2:00 p.m. This approach is well received by consumers, and in the case of the furniture company Hanssem한샘, they sold Sam Bookcase and Sam Kids Organizer two million sets and one million sets respectively after introducing the service.[1]

Subscription Service for Optimal Satisfaction

In addition to faster delivery service, efforts are being made to provide optimized satisfaction to end customers at the last mile. In particular, companies are launching subscription delivery service for a wide variety of categories to meet the demands of customers who buy certain products on a regular basis but find it troublesome to remember to place the order before they run out. According to Shinhan Card's Big Data Research Institute신한카드 빅데이터연구소, cosmetics accounted for the highest share in the subscription category. For example, AmorePacific's product, Steady스테디 is available via a subscription service that delivers the four-stage mask packs within a span of five days for consumers who has the skincare regimen of using one mask pack a day.

Coupang쿠팡, an online commerce company famous for its rocket delivery, is also offering next-morning delivery service while expanding its subscription service particularly for daily necessity items. Now, Coupang customers can have diapers and powdered milk, cosmetics and vitamins, and even pet food delivered to them on a regular basis. Currently, Coupang boasts over 400,000 subscription members.

Other popular subscription items include razors and female sanitary pads, and Weekly Shirts위클리셔츠 offers a subscription service that delivers 3~5 laundered and ironed shirts every week to its subscription customers.

2. Last Fit in Mobility

In the last fit economy, the center of the economic world is "near my house." The so-called "All-in-One Village", a village that has all the necessary infrastructure for daily activities such as shopping, leisure and cultural activities within 10 minutes walking distance from home, is emerging as a new residential trend. Thanks to this trend, big changes are happening in the commercial zone within an apartment complex, which in the past was only perceived as an accessory to the apartment complex. The number of common businesses such as real estate agents, beauty parlors, and after-school academies are on a decline, while the number of restaurants and cultural, art, and entertainment businesses are experiencing a sharp increase in the neighborhood residential facility zone. Many of these neighborhood businesses are emerging as hot spots that represent the area.

The growing importance of neighborhood living zones that offer easier mobility has brought about changes in services offered by convenience stores. Competition over new service offers is fierce among many convenience store franchises such as CU (lunch box, beverage, and fruit delivery, bill payment, used phone collection), GS25 (laundry pick-up, charging and parking electric scooters, free access to medical devices), 7-Eleven (home shopping order returns, overseas document delivery), and E-Mart 24 (wine order payment and pick-up).

As the last fit economic trend of taking care of all daily needs near the house shows a noticeable change, regional-based second-hand trading platforms have also been recording a rapid growth. In the case of Danggeun Market당근마켓 that launched in 2015, it recorded less than one million visitors for the first three years, but beginning in mid-2018, it has enjoyed a J-shaped rapid growth curve on the graph. Their growth grabbed the attention of venture capitals including Softbank Ventures that invested 6.8 billion won in 2018 as well as Altos Ventures that invested 40 billion won in September 2019.[2] This rise of the last fit economy can be attributed to the consumption trend in which people wish to minimize the effort, time, and cost they put into mobility and enjoy a more relaxed life instead.

Golden Age of Scooters and the Last Fit Mobility

The mobile services that utilize personal transportation vehicles such as electric scooters and bicycles can be defined as "the last fit mobility." Recent growth in the electronic scooter market is a good example for the growing demand for the last fit mobility. The importance of a simple operation method and speedy mobility is growing noticeably as well while the range of customers' activities is narrowing down to the vicinity of their homes.

That is the reason IT companies are eagerly investing in electric scooter sharing services in each country. Google and Uber in the U.S. have invested $335 million in Lime, a company specializing in electric scooters. In Korea, Naver has invested in Go-Go-Ssing고고씽, and Socar invested in Elecle일레클.[3] "Kick Going킥고잉," which has attracted investment from Hyundai Motors and Kolon Investment, is currently operating in Seoul and Pangyo in Gyeonggi Province with over 3,000 sharable electric scooters.

Hyundai Motors took the first step ahead of others by launching a personal transportation vehicle sharing service at major tourist attractions on Jeju Island. The company is test operating ZET, which is a last fit mobility platform that customers can use on the last leg on their way to a destina-

The solution that links vehicles and electric scooters will bring the most efficient and perfect last fit mobility for customers from the beginning to the end.

tion after using their own vehicles or public transportation. The company is also considering the option of mounting an electric scooter on a new model vehicle slated to be released in 2021. The Hyundai scooter is relatively lightweight and made to be foldable so that users can keep it inside the vehicle or carry it with them when using public transportation. The solution that links vehicles and electric scooters will bring the most efficient and perfect last fit mobility for customers from the beginning to the end. It is not just Hyundai Motors, either. Other leading global automobile companies such as Volkswagen, Daimler, BMW and Ford, are also showing interest in the last fit mobility as well.

3. The Last Fit in Purchasing Journey

The moment when consumers unpack their orders and touch the products is becoming just as important as the experience of using the products themselves. The unboxing process is the moment when they experience the physical products for the first time, and the moment is filmed with a camera. It's been a while since unboxing videos became popular on YouTube.

Recently, the trend went one step further from unboxing and gave birth to the term "haul." Haul is about people purchasing certain products, introducing them to their video viewers, and sharing their honest reviews. They add the word "haul" to the brand, product, or the category that they are introducing, such as "travel souvenir haul", "skin toner haul", or "luxury haul".

Given this focus, manufacturers of electric devices are forced to pay as much attention to packaging as to the performance of their products, because the customers' candid reviews cover not just the performance or design of their products, but also their packing and print quality.

For early adopters, packaging boxes as well as products themselves are important aspects of their purchasing experience. Now that the unboxing process has become part of the whole product package, the term OOBE(Out of Box Experience) has emerged in the electric device industry.

Last Trip: Emphasis on the Last Activity

The travel market is also exhibiting the phenomenon of optimizing the last-minute experience. Nowadays, consumer satisfaction does not simply depend on the travel location, but it depends on the experiences people had during their trip. Due to this change, "activity tours" that offer various activities during a trip has become much more popular for the last 4-5 years. For example, the travel industry is now offering "Roman Home-Style Cooking Classes" instead of "Rome Tours," and "Small Group Carp Fishing in London" instead of "London Tours". These new t travel is created in accordance with the travelers' interests. In the past, touring as many regions as possible over a long period of time was popular, but lately, people tend to prefer concentrating on one region over a brief period.

The travel platforms that focus on selling activity products, such as My Real Trip, WAUG and Klook are attracting young consumers and recording three to five times their growth in sales last year.[4]

Background for the Last Fit Economy

Changing Criteria for Consumer Rationality

Consumer rationality can be either objective or subjective. Objective rationality refers to the act of maximizing objective utility. The utility described here means the satisfaction gained by consuming goods, and it is usually determined by the degree of satisfaction in proportion to the input resources. If the objective utility is high, that means these three conditions are satisfied: when the price is low; when the performance is excellent; and when the brand has a good value When the level of satisfaction is high on all of these three conditions, consumers are perceived to have a high level of objective rationality.

Recently, however, subjective rationality has started to matter more. In the last fit economy, sensory and subjective utility often dominates consumer rationality. In other words, low scores on objective measures may have little to do with actual consumer satisfaction. Utility is not simply evaluated based on the efficient use of monetary resources, and the impact of subjective satisfaction on utility is growing. This implies that even when objective utility is rather low, services can increase their subjective utility by satisfying customers at the last mile and eventually increase the overall rationality level. As the criteria for rationality change,

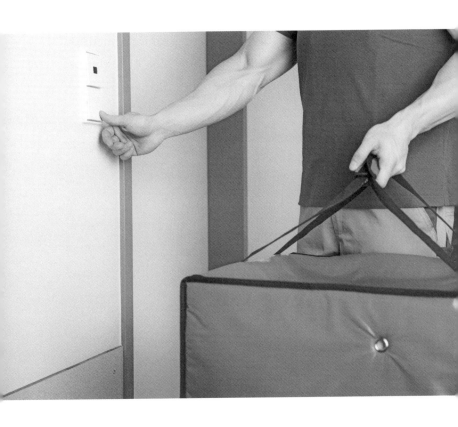

Customer satisfaction at the point
of contact where products meet customers
is more important than product
performance itself.
Those who seize that last minute
will seize the market.

the focus of competition is changing from competition over which product is better to competition over who can provide better customer satisfaction at the last mile with increased convenience and speed.

Changes in Household Types and Generation Characteristics

Changes following the increasing number of one-to-two-person households also had a lot of impact on consumption behavior. As the household unit grows smaller, the unit of consumption began to grow smaller as well, consequently leading consumers to become convenience-oriented rather than objective efficiency-oriented. More than anything, almost all single-person households are engaged in economic activities, and they naturally opt for more time-saving services. In many cases, consumers also turn to the services of the last fit economy to make up for the shortage of family members. For one-person household members who do not own a car, carrying heavy grocery bags from the mart to home is a lot of trouble in itself, and even if they own a car, they might find it depressing to shop for groceries alone in the mart. Next-morning delivery or subscription delivery services are some of the good examples of accurately meeting the needs of these single-person households.

Generational characteristics also contribute to the spread

of the last fit economy. As millennials and generation Z have entered into society, the growth of these services has also been accelerating. Generation Z, in particular, pursues subjective utility, which gives them immediate happiness, rather than economic utility. Therefore, it is no coincidence that the last fit economy began to spread just around the time when Generation Z began to make their entry into society. In addition, since Generation Z belongs to the Phono-Sapiens who are savvy with mobile and online, they tend to seek untact services more than other forms of services. They choose the untact type as one of the conditions for optimized satisfaction, while avoiding unnecessary and consuming interpersonal relationships.

Implications

The optimized satisfaction that today's consumers want is the "value" that goes beyond the product's usefulness or performance. In other words, the criteria for customer satisfaction are shifting from performance-oriented evaluations to value-oriented evaluations. Besides the performance, price, or brand image of products, the convenient experiences the products provide have become an important factor in consumption behavior, and this behavior is expected to grow at an accelerating speed. It means the experience of service that leads to the optimized satisfaction at the last mile becomes more important. The customer needs are evolving into specialized services that save their labor and time while promising convenience most importantly, a systematic delivery system that brings fresher products faster to the customers, and a satisfying experience in the last mile. So, what should companies consider to ensure optimal customer satisfaction?

The important issue in the distribution market is moving towards customer satisfaction experiences, instead of just fast delivery.

In the logistics market, the key factor for competitiveness used to be cost optimization. However, today's key factor is customer satisfaction. Therefore, in the last fit economy, David can become competitive enough to vie with Goliath as long as David can offer satisfying customer experiences. In order to respond to the consumption ecosystem where revolutionary changes are expected, companies need to come up with strategies to maximize customers' subjective utility by providing excellent experiences in the last mile and saving customers' time as much as possible.

In order to successfully employ the last fit economy strategies, businesses have to be able to provide optimized customer satisfaction that takes environmental issues into consideration. Lately, distribution industry insiders claim that fast delivery is essential, and now, the age of competition over eco-friendly delivery has dawned, because the war in the delivery market brought about serious environment pollution problems caused by packaging materials. Distribution companies are taking such measures as supplying reusable cooler bags or introducing eco-friendly electric vehicles that do not emit exhaust fumes. In the last fit economy, environmental issues must be addressed, and under no circumstances should the environment be compromised for the sake of convenience.

Ultimately, the kernel of the last fit economy is differentiated services. Strategies for delivery optimization, time optimization, and experience optimization all use differentiation as their main weapon. Businesses that play a "money game" and use existing infrastructure efficiently may have a leg up and get established fast, but that is not an essential competitive edge that can help businesses survive in the market. This is because consumers expect services that can build more innovative and convenient habits. A differentiating strategy should be devised to keep the business going in an "edgy" manner, not in a common and business-as-usual manner. Just like Market Kurly마켓컬리 that opened the age of next morning delivery, businesses need to think hard about differentiating their services based on innovative and quick thinking skills. In the end, those who seize the customers' last moments and grab the customers' front door knobs will seize the market.

Goodness and Fairness:

Fair Player

The pursuit of goodness and fairness will become stronger.
Employees expect to have their contributions fairly recognized
even if they are at the bottom of the corporate ladder. Domestic
chores must be divided equally among all family members.
Students prefer individual assignments over team projects
and tests with multiple-choice questions over writing essays
on the given subjects. When making purchases, consumers
care about the "good influence" of a brand as well as products
themselves. The "fair players" from the younger generation,
who have grown up in a society where individuality has become
an important value, want to change society through their small

actions in various media. Boycotting campaigns that get ignited whenever relevant issues get raised are not simply a temporary fever of the moment; they express people's desire for fairness, goodness, and effectiveness.

Several reasons can be identified for the growing desire for fairness. First, awareness of discrimination has increased as society has become more equality-oriented. Second, fierce competition has become second nature for the millennial generation, who grew up in economic prosperity but are experiencing the frustration of a low-growth era as well. Third, the self-efficacy of the "fair player generation" has increased because they can voice their opinions thanks to the influential leverage of telecommunication technology that supports real-time interactive communication. At a time of increasing demand for fairness, fair player consumers use purchasing behavior as a form of a "dollar vote."

Therefore, companies need to go beyond simply selling their products and need to consider the environmental and social consequences of their products. The generation that is pursuing fairness more than any other generation is coming into their own.

"What is the percentage pay increase for the executives of our company? Mine is just...."

An HR manager was recently asked this question by a young employee. Evidently, young employees these days want to know more about the salary increase rate of executives in their company than that of their peers or direct bosses. In an interview with the authors, the HR manager, who has years of experience, said that he was quite surprised by that question. The question is indicative of the values of today's young employees, concerned with whether the company's evaluation system is fair. By comparing the salary increase rates, a young employee may wonder, "Is that executive really contributing to the company to justify that pay increase?" or "Am I being treated fairly given the contribution I make to the company?"

The young employee asking about percentage pay increase is not the only one questioning fairness. These days, members of younger generations get particularly angry when they feel fairness is compromised. "Fairness" means, according to the dictionary, behavior without discrimination or bias, usually with regard to how rules or regulations in a system apply impartially to subjects. If young employees suspect that salary increase rates are determined not by performance but by rank, they will feel the difference between their increase rate and an executive's increase rate is unfair. "Equality" is a similar concept to fairness, and the two are sometimes used interchangeably. However, equality has more to do with structural and consequential aspects of a system, whereas fairness has more to do with application of rules in a competitive situation. Imagine you are waiting in a line at a grocery store. If someone cuts in line and is served before you, you will feel "fairness has been violated."

According to MIT professor Richard Larson, fairness is an essential factor in maintaining a stable social system, and is in fact, an instinct that almost every human being has.[1] An experiment conducted at a fast food restaurant showed that consumers prefer to keep to one line even if it means a longer wait rather than forming three to four lines even if it means faster service. It is because they cannot stand those who arrived later than themselves being served faster, even if it means they might have to wait longer. To them, unfair process matters more than their own loss.

The desire for fairness, which used to be considered a social structure issue, is now creating new lifestyles throughout society. Domestic chores have to be fairly distributed to all family members, and students prefer multiple-choice exams to short-answer exams, as well as individual assignments to team projects. In the workplace, employees want to be evaluated based on their own job performance rather than supporting their team leaders, and even the lowest-ranking employees would engage in conversation with the top management executive as casually as if they are friends. When buying products, the righteous and "good influence" of the brand matters just as much as the products themselves. These consumers who seek fairness in all areas of their daily lives can be called "fair players."

Shouting Fairness from the Top of the World

Orienting Toward a Function-centered Horizontal Relationship

"Managing director? I don't find him difficult. Honestly, I'm more comfortable with him because I don't need to kowtow to him to impress him."

It might sound a little shocking, but any young office worker who is currently working for a company may sympathize with this. Young people these days sure don't seem to be "afraid of the executives" compared to older generations. They don't get nervous when they are with their bosses, and they don't feel the need to act more respectful than necessary. They don't seem to be intimidated by their authority, and in fact, they seem as comfortable to be with them as with their next door neighbors. But if you look a little deeper, it's not a very strange at all. "What's the difference between the managing director and me?" they say. But just because they don't feel the intimidated by higher-ranking bosses doesn't mean they are not respectful of them. For them, a managing director is paid more because he has heavier responsibilities in the company. Therefore, they don't feel the need to become servile and grovel before them more than necessary as if they are in a master and servant relationship.

Desire for this kind of "fair relationship" is spreading throughout society. The conventional age and seniori-ty-based hierarchical relationships are now replaced by ca-pability-based horizontal relationships. People today don't place more emphasis than necessary on their relationships either. For them, it is fair for you to get better treatment than others if you have the skills that are essential in a cer-tain situation, even if you are at the bottom of the corporate ladder.

In a way, it is a thoroughly function-oriented mindset. This change in mindset is also bringing about changes in the work process as well. For example, even if you are an executive boss, you are not supposed to unilaterally command your subordinates to carry out a given job assignment. If you tell them, "This job is assigned to you.

So, there are no but's or if's. Just do it," this is the worst kind of communication. You are supposed to explain convincingly, such as the reason a certain subordinate is assigned to a specific job, and how his/her contribution will manifest in what form. The atmosphere seems to be that senior workers cannot ask even the newest worker to do the things that used to be accepted as natural part of the work routine for new hires. Such minor tasks as printing out or putting together presentations for a conference meeting might be fully acceptable as a favor, but things that have nothing to do with work, such as asking for a cup of coffee, is becoming a thing of the past.

Horizontal relationships among corporate members are also reflected in arranging workspaces within the company. In the past, the executives had their desks somewhere far from the entrance, by the window or in other prime locations that had a good view, while the new hires had their desks closer to the hallway that had heavy employee traffic. In the past, the higher the ranking, the bigger the desks and furniture you got. But now, many companies are revamping this hierarchy-based office space arrangement.

In June 2019, the furniture maker Fursys퍼시스 launched a system in which employees are allowed to pick their own workspace in the company to test a new office environment culture. The company allows employees to work in the environment that they want, depending on the daily work

In a new office environment culture, everyone uses furniture of the same specs called "universal furniture" regardless of rank or position of team leaders or team members.

situation, instead of specifically designating where their workspace should be. The employees can choose to work in a room for one or two persons where they can work alone, and it is also possible to work in a cafe, lounge, or rest area. The seats by the windows, which used to be the exclusive domain of executives, are now occupied by ordinary employees.[2] It is also noteworthy that everyone uses furniture of the same specs called "universal furniture" regardless of rank or position of team leaders or team members.

Gender Roles Based on Differences Instead of Discrimination

At home, the relationship between a husband and wife began to evolve to become equal. A good example of trends among young couples who are about to get married is "half-and-half wedding expenses." In the past, the groom was supposed to pay for the housing expenses while the bride was supposed to pay for all furniture and appliances, but this wedding approach is now considered old-fashioned. The young generation today strives to equally foot the financial burden of marriage regardless of gender. Of course, it doesn't mean an exact split of 50:50. It is open for discussion between the couple depending on the situation, so that the one who is more financially ready takes more financial burden, be it the groom or the bride.

The share of household chores between couples is also changing. The role of a father used to be supporting the family through economic activities while the role of a mother used to be taking care of the children, but now, couples are leaving these stereotyped roles behind and their roles are up for change depending on the circumstances of the family. The change is slow, but it is becoming a part of the family culture itself. For example, young couples today make joint decisions regarding their children's education. According to a company specializing in children's education, when their counselors discuss children's education issues with mothers, one of the most frequent responses from the mothers these days is, "I will discuss the issue with my husband and get back to you." It is because, for couples today, education for their children is not solely the wife's responsibility, but the couple's shared responsibility. The number of husbands in charge of kitchen work such as cooking and washing dishes has also increased. According to a residential interior company, when young housewives are remodeling their kitchens these days, a surprising number of them ask the company to raise the sink to match the height of their husbands since it is mostly used by their husbands.

Contracts and Manuals Matter

"Young employees these days rarely greet me when they see me in the company elevator, they just look at their cell phones. When I was a new hire, I used to bow to my seniors....."

This is what corporate seniors often say these days. There are even young employees who openly ignore their seniors in the elevator. However, their actions have their own reasons. For them, elevators are not yet part of the company, and their work life begins only when they sit at their desks with their earbuds on. Earbuds are not just a device for listening to music. They are a shield that makes them "private individuals" from the external world. If the job contract stipulates that the working hours are from 9 a.m. to 6 p.m., they need to start their job assignment at the strike of 9 a.m. To them, advice from the boss to come to work half an hour early to get ready for the day is just nagging.

For today's employees, only the facts written down in the contract are the criteria of fairness. Therefore, it is against fairness to demand a sense of responsibility that is beyond what is written in the contract. Having a full guarantee of a lunch hour is also their right that has to be protected in accordance with the contract terms. This is the reason they refuse to have lunch with their bosses when asked and prefer enjoying lunch time on their own.

The way employees act demanding fairness might look rather selfish to older generations, but that doesn't mean they are less committed to their work. When necessary, they don't mind working overtime at night or even weekends to do their best for their job assignments. If there is anything different from the past, they tally the overtime hours that they've worked for a month and rightfully demand vacation time that is equivalent to their overtime tally. Instead of just making sacrifices for the company, they make sure to demand compensation for the efforts they've put in for the company as well. Since they can be fairly acknowledged for the efforts they invest for the company, they have less work stress resulting from having to night-shift or overtime, and it sometimes leads to improved work efficiency as well.

The Evaluation System Must be Equal for All

If there is something students these days hate, it is team projects. In the past, students preferred assignments to tests, and they particularly preferred team projects. In fact, there are many advantages to team projects, which require them to collaborate with each other as a team and finish the project together. Team members can exchange ideas with each other and develop a thinking process. In fact, it can be a good learning experience about group life because when they enter society, they are often required to carry out work assignments as a team.

The most fundamental reason students hate team projects is the "free-rider" that always exists within a team. A team being a kind of community that shares the same destiny, those in the team who do not proactively participate in the project are given the same credit as other team members who do. College students these days find this process itself very unfair. What they want is a fair assessment of the capabilities and the effort they put in. If there are no clear criteria of assessment, and if their contributions are not fully recognized, they are not happy because it is deemed unfair to them. For this reason, recent college students prefer individual tasks to group assignments and multiple-choice exams to short-answer exams. There is also a change in how a team is put together for a group project. In the past, students wanted to form a group with their close friends.

But nowadays, students ask their teacher to randomly create teams. It is because students think randomness is the most fair method for everybody.

What is more important than anything else to ensure fairness is whether an objective evaluation is possible without subjective factors being involved. The important point here is, "Can we apply a fair evaluation system to everyone without giving special favors to a particular person?" In a similar context, people can watch sports such as running, swimming, and curling more comfortably than those where referees or judges are involved, such as soccer, baseball, and figure skating. The recent trend of accepting the video review system in refereed games such as soccer and baseball without feeling repulsed about it is deeply related to this trend.

Background of the Growing Importance of Fairness

Koreans' Awareness of Equality

The Incheon International Airport in Korea boasts a reputation as a world-class airport, but there is one thing the airport lacks: a fast track. Most airports around the world, including London's Heathrow International Airport and Paris' Charles de Gaulle Airport, operate a fast track system that allows speedy arrival and departure procedures for first-class passengers. In Korea, however, attempts to introduce the system have repeatedly failed because of the concerns that it might foster a sense of socio-economic disparities.

As one can see from this airport example, contemporary Koreans are known to have a strong awareness of equality. Which raises the question: why are Koreans so conscious about equality? It may be due to the fact that the high population density of the county makes people more sensitive to social comparisons and that the dramatic and rapid changes in Korean society in the last 100 years have resulted in extreme changes in people's social status and achievement, with some people obtaining relatively higher social status and better achievement than others. Some point out that it is due to the widening inequality of wealth and the consequential class inequality that has been deepening in Korean society. Of course, it is not entirely wrong, but it is a stretch to apply it to our society as it is, because some argue that inequality in Korean society has gradually improved compared to the past. In fact, in a paper published in 2019, Jeong In-kwan and Park Hyun-joon revealed that the correlation between the parental socio-economic status and that of their children has gradually decreased due to increased investment in education and increased opportunities in Korean society.[3] Those who were born in 1950~1984 experienced more rapid socio-economic mobility than the previous or following generations did according to the paper.

What really matters is not the objective size of the wealth gap. We need to pay more attention to the fact that the sense of "lack of fairness" is growing stronger despite the gradual improvement in the wealth gap in Korea. With regard to this problem, there is a paradoxical argument that people's desire for fairness has increased because inequality in society has decreased. According to Alexis de Tocqueville, a French political thinker from the first half of the 19th century, there was no concern about discrimination in feudal times when the difference in social classes was preconditioned, because people did not even bother to compare their situation with others.[4] On the other hand, he argued, when social systems advance and the structural discrimination based on social classes are abolished, the issue of fairness begins to surface because anyone can, in theory, enjoy the possibility of belonging to the upper class.

Tocqueville's point reveals the fundamental contradictions we are destined to face when we pursue a fair society. If our society is completely fair, there is no excuse for those in the lower groups of population, such as the poor or the failed, to blame society for their downfall, because it could only be interpreted that their fall and failure is attributed to a lack in their own talent or efforts, not to the unfair social system. In this case, if we believe "Our society has a fair criterion of assessment, but the process of applying them is not fair," then we can deny our inferiority. That is the very reason the more we pursue fairness, the stronger our desire for fairness.

Characteristics of Today's Young Generation

Some argue that, in addition to Korea's socio-structural characteristics, the Korean younger generations are more sensitive to fairness than their older counterparts. Born between the early 1980s and the late 1990s, the millennial generation grew up enjoying economic prosperity and quality educational opportunities in the post-ideological conflict era. However, they also witnessed fierce competition among countries racing for free trade and globalization. In particular, millennials, who have experienced the financial crisis of 2008 and the subsequent period of low-growth and low interest, are considered as "the first generation poorer than their parents."

Competition is the main keyword that dominates the lives of the younger generation in Korea. They went through fierce competition for college admission in their teens and endless job-hunting competition in their 20s, and in their 30s and onward, they continue to compete with others for job promotion to survive in the company. The most important value for today's younger generation to survive the age of bottomless meritocracy is none other than competition secured by fairness. It is because, while

The most important value for today's younger generation to survive the age of bottomless meritocracy is none other than competition secured by fairness. They are most angry at those who are given a free pass to success.

producing results through one's own efforts is a personal issue, privileges given to certain people regardless of efforts is a matter of fairness on a social level. Therefore, they are most angry at those who are given a free pass to success while habitually engaging in unfair activities thanks to their personal connections and their wealthy parents' money.

That is the reason why students these days welcome a college admission system that primarily uses standardized test scores but they oppose a system that uses a broader range of information about academic and extra-curricular performance. For the same reason, students prefer a test with multiple choice questions over a test with short answer questions. It is because the only type of tests that they can fairly challenge with their own industrious efforts without the support or background of a wealthy family is standardized multiple choice tests. The fact that not only publicly owned companies but also private companies are increasingly using National Competency Standards (NCS) tests when hiring employees reflects these young fair players' thirst for fairness.

Technological Innovation

Some argue that the desire for fairness is the result of social change caused by technological innovation. They claim that it is not just a characteristic of Korean society, or a characteristic shared only by the younger generation, but a kind of contemporary change that is happening in a similar fashion almost everywhere around the world. In the past, society was dominated by hierarchical organizations where certain groups controlled individuals while monopolizing information, but in the current era where communication through social media on the internet has become widespread, ordinary consumers are generating and spreading information. With the disclosure of information becoming daily routine and an increasing number of ordinary people becoming professionals in various areas, there is a growing demand for truth-based decision making, which in other words, means a need for fairness.

Customers give a low star rating on the internet to unfriendly restaurants, and employees share their candid opinions about their company on online anonymous platforms provided by apps like Blind블라인드. Information that used to be shared within closed networks is now disclosed to the public. Bits of disclosed information can have a decisive impact on people's decision-making and, moreover, they can even reverse the general attitudes of the public.

Therefore, it is natural for today's customers to want to take part in bringing about positive changes in society. Buying a product from a "socially responsible enterprise" used to be just something that brought satisfaction to the individual consumer, but now, it has become the easiest way to exert a good influence on others. The relatively small act of purchasing everyday products can become a way to manifest one's "global citizen identity," as this small act not only provides personal satisfaction but also promotes a more positive society, contributing to positive changes on a global level.

Implications

The fair players' desire for fairness will bring about certain changes in society. First, there will be organizational innovation. The organizational structure of a company will rapidly change into a form such that the members of the company believe the structure is fair. Speed of decision-making and work efficiency will improve as people can work according to their expertise instead of being tied to a seniority-centered vertical hierarchy. The younger generation will become more motivated to work harder with greater passion when the salary scale system changes to be based on people's performance and ability instead of on seniority.

Consumer interference in business activities will become much more powerful. Paul Samuelson, who won the 1995 Nobel Prize in economics, has described consumers' purchasing behavior as a form of "dollar votes." According to him, consumers realize social justice by repeatedly purchasing services and products made by good companies, just like voters contribute by voting to realize a better society. We also need to take notice that the fair players' preference for good companies is creating a kind of fandom when the strength of overall brand loyalty is on the decline. It might have been enough for companies to distinguish their products in terms of ingredients, designs, or other general attributes. However, they now also need to consider the environmental and social consequences of their products and services.

Meanwhile, we should not overlook the negative consequences of fairness as well. One example of the inevitable problems associated with horizontal network organizations is that, unlike in traditional hierarchical organizations, there is no one to take responsibility when something goes wrong. In fact, some critics say that employees these days want to be horizontal in communication but vertical in their responsibilities, and that they are greedy for more work even if they don't have enough resources to perform that additional work. Systematic measures should be found to beef up both the sense of responsibility and professionalism.

From now on, society will need to listen more attentively to the voices of the fair players, who are demanding greater fairness. In fact, it is difficult to grasp the problems we have unless they express what they are not happy about with their organizations and society. Possible measures could include preventing potential problems in advance and discovering unexpected opportunities by providing them with a platform where they can make comments on whatever they consider to be unfair at any time.

Here and Now

the 'Streaming Life'

Not just in the way people listen to music, but the way of life itself is changing from downloading to streaming. Streaming technology plays audio or video through a network, and it has the advantage of allowing people to experience content without having to download and own it. Having grown accustomed to streaming, consumers now want to apply this technology to every aspect of life. First, they stream their living space, realizing their dreams and designing their lifestyles comprehensively. That is, they experience a wide variety of lifestyles by staying in different conceptual spaces in a neighborhood they want to live in for a period of time they want. Second, they also stream hobbies or leisure activities by subscribing to expert recommendations. People receive style recommendations that suit their tastes, and they subscribe to cosmetics services that suit their skin type and have the products delivered on a regular basis. Lastly, people stream by borrowing. Instead of applying mental effort to select one item, they rent all the options and try them all out. People can rent anything including their dream cars, luxury handbags, and furniture items.

Accounting for this spread of streaming life are today's younger generation — with their inflated desires but limited resources — and their floating nomadic lifestyle. Another factor behind this trend is the technological development that accelerates the transition from owning products, services, spaces and experiences to streaming them all. People today collect the scenes of their daily lives, which are lighthearted but enriching. In order to meet the demands of these people, a new grammar of the market is called for. As customers stream products and services instead of purchasing them in one transaction to own, it will increasingly become more important for businesses to embrace a relationship centered approach where they manage their customer's entire "streaming journey."

As indicated by the word itself, "streaming" is a content transmission method that allows music, drama, movies, novels and other content items to be played real time without downloading them from the internet. The concept was first introduced in 1995 at Real Audio developed by Real Network Inc. The key point of this technology is giving users access to content items so that they can enjoy the contents any time they want without having to own them. A music source service is probably one of the most commonly used streaming services in daily routines, but lately, in response to the wide distribution of video content products, various over-the-top (OTT) services such as Netflix, Apple TV, Watcha Play and Wave are offering content streaming services as well.

Noteworthy is the fact that streaming services that have started with content products are now expanding to other products. Now, people can easily replace durable goods, such as electronic appliances, couches, or beds, without having to hold on to them for years. People can also have products of their choice delivered to the door on a regular basis.

Furthermore, more and more people are using streaming services even for their workplace or residential spaces, showing how the paradigm of consuming clothing, food, housing and leisure is changing from ownership to usership. Now, the amount of experience rather than the amount of possession becomes a new way of measuring one's affluence.

Life streaming covers a variety of consumer activities including renting products instead of purchasing to own them and subscription membership in which they pay money to get recommendations for goods and services for a certain period of time. The key point here is not owning products, but the possibility of having diverse experiences through streaming. Just as music lovers used to fill their shelves with LPs, consumers today fill their lives with streaming experiences. What matters is not how much you own. The emergence of streaming life suggests a shift of paradigm from ownership to usership.

From Ownership to Streaming

In his book, *The Age of Access*, Jeremy Rifkin predicted that the era of ownership would go, and the age of access would come. According to him, people would request and use products or capital only when necessary, instead of owning and managing them by themselves. In this sense, Jeremy Rifkin defines that the opposite of ownership is access, not non-ownership. Twenty years after the book was published, the era of access and experience that Jeremy Rifkin predicted is unfolding at full speed.

In traditional ownership life, "exchange value" was important because the act of purchasing took place only when a product was worth the price. In addition, ownership was important because ownership meant being an asset. In ownership life, people usually used a product until the end of its life cycle. On the other hand, "experience value" is more important in streaming life, because the key to streaming life lies in the journey of accumulating experiences by using, enjoying, and feeling various products and services. Products are not really important as an asset. What is important is the right to access or the right to use various products and services so that people can have diverse experiences. In ownership life, people used products until the end of their life cycle. But in streaming life, people use products until the access right expires. Since the consumption period is limited to a certain range of time, streaming consumers tend to prefer customized services that allow them to express their own tastes and lifestyles more than before.

Therefore, in the era of streaming life, the journey you have with products, services, and content items that you stream becomes a barometer that shows your taste. Now, we will look at the experience journey of streaming consumers who collect experiences through streaming and reveal their identity through the experiences, and the background and implications of the emergence of streaming life.

Various Lifestyles in Streaming Life

Life Backpackers:

Space-Subscribing Lifestyle Streaming

One of the most popular content items offered by the American digital media company Refinery29 is *Sweet Digs* which shows the lifestyles of America's most hip and young consumers.[1] In five to eight minutes of short video, this show tells stories of people living in the cities that are popular among young people, such as New York and Los Angeles. A typical character in this video is someone who pays a monthly rent of $3,000 for a small apartment in Brooklyn and lives a minimalist lifestyle. These people are unwilling to leave Brooklyn or Los Angeles, even if they have to share an apartment with a housemate to split their monthly rent of $7,500. Despite the murderous housing costs, they do not give up living in Brooklyn or Los Angeles, because there is cultural diversity that can be enjoyed only there. There is information that is only available in Brooklyn, and there is an inspiration that is naturally acquired from people and interactions with them that can only be met in Brooklyn. There are values and lifestyles that they cannot have access to anywhere else. So, for them, home is not property, nor is it a settlement. A house is only a platform through which they share their stories with others and fill daily episodes with new experiences.

Recently, there has been a growing interest in residential or commercial spaces that people can experience. Good examples of this new business are shared houses or shared offices that feature expanded common areas and minimized personal spaces. If you buy a membership and become a member of the community, you can experience diverse cultural atmospheres in the community by interacting with other community members. You can even subscribe to a space in a different country so you can experience that space while traveling. Since the main concept is "using" instead of "buying" or "leasing" a space, you can subscribe to other spaces that you want to try out any time you want.

One of the characteristics of lifestyle-streaming shared spaces is that these spaces are concentrated in neighborhoods they want to live in, and in the commercial districts where they want to work. For example, the Korean branches of WeWork are mostly concentrated in the Jongno, Gangnam, and Yeoksam area, Seoul. Another example is Common Town커먼타운, which is a shared house brand of Kolon House Vision that started with three branches in 2017. As of May 2019, the Common Town branches have increased to 33, most of which are concentrated in Apgujeong, Cheongdam-dong, Samsung-dong, and other neighborhoods in Gangnam District. The social apartment "the t'able," which is run by SK D&D, is located near Exit 4 of the Gangnam subway station, which is known for being one of the highest rents in Korea. These are businesses that appeal to urban dwellers who want to look posh even if they work only one day and want to live in a hip neighborhood even if they live there for only a month. They cannot afford a house or office in an urban center, but if they stream those spaces, it is almost the same as having realized their dreams.

Another advantage of shared space is that users have access to common spaces that are not possible when they live alone. It is like having 3~4 living rooms designed in different concepts within the same housing unit, just like drivers who make a monthly payment to drive many different car models. Therefore, residential sharing services emphasize common areas designed under different concepts or attract people who dream of enjoying such areas. Some of the examples include living room space designed like a cafe or a member exclusive activity room where members can take classes on meditation and yoga. Other examples include entertainment space where members can play games and a rooftop terrace where barbeques are available. These are the facilities that members have access to and enjoy, even though they have to share with others instead of having it all to themselves. It means, depending on which concept of space you choose, your daily activities might also change.

Residential sharing services emphasize common areas designed under different concepts or attract people who dream of enjoying such areas.

As space begins to reflect a lifestyle, the standards for choosing a room and the length of time staying in that room are also changing. Traditionally, some of the key factors in determining the price of a house were the size, location, and structure of rooms. These standards are important in space streaming as well, but residents consider the lifestyle and taste that suits them in terms of function and design to be the priorities. One good example is the Tree House트리 하우스 that offers six different lifestyle spaces including a cat life concept space that has a built in cat tower and cat walk for cat owners; nomad concept space with built in modular organizing spaces for the nomadic urban dwellers; and minimal concept space that offers a bathtub by minimizing other functions of the space.

The contract period is also getting shorter. Subscribers to such residential services prefer shorter-term contracts and wish to be able to terminate them at any time. The British residential service The Collective Old Oak offers four-month short-term contracts, while Zoku in the Netherlands offers stays as short as just one day like a hotel.

The new tribe that streams their lifestyle breaks down the boundaries of residences as well. German rental housing service Goquaters aims to become one community-multiple locations. By establishing a global membership network, users can pick a place to live in any location as long as Goquaters member companies are located there.

Japan's ADDress, which launched a pilot service in April 2019, is a multi-base co-living service. If you pay an annual membership fee of 40,000 yen per month and a monthly membership fee of 50,000 yen, you can use various bases within Japan at a fixed price. In fact, the increasing number of Japanese people constantly moving from one place to another has given birth to a newly coined term, "Adores Hopper."

Taste Collectors: Recommendation Streaming, Experts' Tastes Delivered to Your Door

The second way to collect experience is to get recommendations from experts. Streaming consumers want a more specialized personal experience that is different from others. That is the background of the emerging streaming services that let consumers select styles curated by experts or have them delivered regularly. This is new concept streaming that allows interior consultants, personal shoppers and sommeliers to recommend products that suit your taste and even deliver them to your home.

The American startup Hooch offers a service where you pay $9.99 a month and you can enjoy a cocktail a day at one of the hundreds of bars in Manhattan. Korea's Daily Shot데일리샷 is a similar service. This service, which allows you to have a drink per day for free in any of the bars within its network for 9,900 won per month, welcomed 5,000 members who signed up in the year after launching.[2] Other popular services include having wine experts such as a sommelier select wines based on the members' personal taste and deliver wine once a month or deliver traditional liquor in a similar fashion. They provide not only alcohol, but also a variety of information such as instructions on how to taste the wine or liquor, food to pair with them, and alcohol-related histories.

The New Rental Tribe: Streaming to Rent and Experiencing Your Own Tastes and Choices

Many of us have the bitter experience of spending significant time and money on buying a new couch or car only to find out a better model is being released soon after. To avoid these situations, streaming consumers choose to "rent" rather than buy a product. When the rental period of a product is over, they "stream" another product.

The rental services that streaming consumers use are different from the usual traditional rental services. Conventional rental services usually require a contract with a long rental period, and they have limited items available. But the new rental tribe does not want long-term rentals. For that reason, the latest rental market is moving in a direction where the rental period is relatively short, and more diverse items are available for rental.

The limit in the items available for rentals is also disappearing. In particular, there is a trend in which durable consumer goods, which people used to buy and use for more than ten years, are quickly join the list of items available for rental. One good example is automobile.

When Volvo launched a service called "Care by Volvo" in the U.S. in September 2017, it put a rather provocative phrase on the front page ad, saying, "Don't buy this car." Care by Volvo is a service that allows you to use four car models including a compact SUV model XC40 at the cost of $750 to $850 monthly payment, and you can use the service without extra deposit or registration fees. Volvo plans to have half of the cars they manufacture available for similar subscription services by 2025.[3]

In Korea, Hyundai Motor has launched the "Hyundai Selection", which lets you pick and drive Sonata, Tucson or Veloster at the cost of 720,000 won per month. If you sign up for this, you can pick from the larger SUV Palisade, Grand Starex limousine and Kona Electric and drive it four 48 hours every month. Kia Motors introduced "Kia Flex Premium," which let you choose from K9, Stinger, and Canibal High limousine once a month to drive that vehicle at the cost of 1,290,000 won monthly subscription fee. These programs attract consumers' attention because they give you an opportunity to drive various car models for a short time. In a way, they rent not because they need them, but because they are curious about them. Streaming services are available for high-end luxury vehicles as well. For example, Genesis Spectrum, which was released by Genesis, is a service you can subscribe to experience high-end sedans. If you pay 1,450,000 won monthly subscription fee, you can pick from three car models — the mid-size sedan G70, subcompact sedan G80, and G80 Sports — and drive it up to two cars each month.

Virtually every kind of vehicles is becoming available for streaming services. For example, Uber launched Uber

Hyundai Motor has launched the "Hyundai Selection," which is popular among consumers in their 30's.

Copter, and as indicated by the name, it is a service that lets you rent a helicopter. If you use this service, you can fly from Manhattan to JFK international airport in New York in just eight minutes at the cost of $200 per ride.[4] You can also Uber submarines as well. Uber introduced the world's first submarine-sharing service, scUber, for about a month in Australia. If you pay for this service, you can take a ride in this mini underwater vehicle and enjoy the famous coral reefs of Cairns and Great Barrier Reef at the bottom of the ocean. When launching the submarine service, Uber declared, "you will be able to enjoy the sight of the world's finest coral reefs while moving through Uber to other destination."[5] Uber is about to transform from a mere transportation service to an experience streaming service that aims to provide an unforgettable memory.

Background of Streaming Life

According to an analysis by the *Harvard Business Review*, more than 11 million consumers in the U.S. use their services in streaming form as of 2017, accounting for about 15 percent of all e-businesses. McKinsey also pointed out that streaming services have been growing 100 percent every year over the past five years.[6] Then the question is: Why is streaming life spreading so fast?

Growing Desires, Declining Resources

Most of the newcomers to streaming life are millennials. The first reason millennials are turning to streaming services is that they don't have enough assets to own the things that they want. The millennials are the first generation in history who are expected to be poorer than their parent generation. When you own something, you need money not just to buy it, but also extra money to maintain it, not to mention time and efforts. So, they choose to have diverse experiences that they can get at reasonable cost instead of buying and owning products and services.

Giving up ownership does not necessarily mean less desire. Having grown up with high-end experiences, millennials have sophisticated tastes. They want to satisfy quantitative desire to have a variety of experiences and the qualitative desire to have higher-quality experiences. A look into the age distribution of members of Hyundai's Selection and Genesis subscription programs reveal that those in their 30s are the biggest age group.[7] In the case of Hyundai Selection, the subscribers in their 30s account for 40 percent of subscribers, and the same age group accounts for 49.7 percent in the case of the Genesis Spectrum. This trend indicates that streaming is becoming a more realistic compromise because they have costly desires they cannot afford to realize them all. Besides, streaming for them is a means to embody their various experiences. In an environment where people can boast their experiences and tastes, it is more efficient to show off their daily routines that are filled with different experiences in social media than owning a single expensive product in reality. This is why experiencing different cars is becoming more important than owning one expensive car.

Values of Nomads with a Drifting Lifestyle

The driving force behind the trend of life streaming is the "nomads," or the values of the nomads who are constantly drifting around instead of settling in one place. The life of modern people who are not afraid to break down boundaries in life share a lot with the nomadic people. Therefore, they want to have access to services at anytime, anywhere, but they also want to be able to hop on to different streaming services at any time as well. The liberal lifestyle that breaks down the boundaries of time and space is the factor that accelerates the transition into streaming life.

The growing number of freelancing jobs also gave rise and growth of the housing streaming that allows people to move around to different bases. According to a survey, Generation Z who are often defined as a digital nomadic population, has an average of 17 jobs, five occupations and 15 residences in their lifetime. That shows how the nomadic values, not some peculiar tastes, are becoming the important keyword that defines the modern people.

The Platform Economy That Makes Streaming Possible

In the past, there were limits to items and brands that can be rented for personal use, but with the proliferation of online-based platform, consumers have the freedom to rent or subscribe almost all services that they need in life in terms of clothing, food, housing and leisure. Also, with the variety of platforms available to connect suppliers and consumers as well as consumers and consumers, the number of players in the streaming market has been growing, consequently accelerating the spread of streaming life. Added to these trends are the online commerce, big data and cloud technologies, all of which serve as a catalyst for the growth of customized streaming life.

In streaming, consumers are purchasing the right to use instead of the right to own, and therefore it is possible to

Having grown accustomed to streaming, consumers now want to apply this technology to every aspect of life. Accounting for this spread of streaming life are today's younger generation – with their inflated desires and limited resources – and their floating nomadic lifestyle.

track each individual consumer's consumption pattern. This data can be analyzed to make recommendations on products or services based on their consumption tendency. Systems that use computer algorithms to make recommendations are attractive to both consumers and service providers. That is the reason numerous streaming service providers are investing on digital intelligence that collects and processes such data.

Implications

As the consumption paradigm is shifting from ownership to experience, streaming services will continue to grow, and more diverse forms of products will become available for streaming. Consumers will soon be able to stream not just cars, furniture items and clothes, but practically everything except for family members and friends. At a time when people even stream houses, businesses need a new way of thinking that breaks the existing framework.

First, the focus of businesses need to shift from sales to customer management. In the ownership-oriented life, post-purchase management of a product is primarily the consumer's responsibility. But in streaming life, businesses have to continuously pay attention to products while consumers are streaming, because streaming is built on the "relationship" between businesses and their consumers. This relationship can be terminated any time if consumers are not satisfied. Experts say that buying a streaming service is just the beginning of a relationship. A continuous relationship between the company and the user has to be maintained by carefully managing post-purchase user experience.

In terms of relationship, space streaming services play more than just a role of renting out space: They can help the "growth" of the residents who use the streaming space. For example, the shared housing service, Life on Together, is geared towards helping residents to develop positive habits, if only minor ones, while living there. For example, housemates help each other to develop a habit of getting up early in the morning or certify a housemate having read one page or more each day. Companies will need such strategies that comprehensively consider and care about the entire life of consumers who have relationship with the company.

Second, quality management of product is important because the products available for streaming services are expanding to expensive durable consumer goods. That means, companies need to ensure the products are in intact conditions when they are returned. Streaming service providers will need to provide with proper manuals and rules, but good manners of streaming service consumers are just as necessary.

Third, companies need to focus their resources on the

curation for individual consumers, not unspecified multiple consumers. In streaming business, service providers are able to obtain accurate knowledge about their customers. That means, they can track the consumption patterns of the consumers who are streaming their products. In the long run, customized service based on the data of consumption patterns should be a differentiation strategy. According to the McKinsey report, subscription services that recommend products or services optimized for each individual consumer recorded 32 percent of subscription service renewal rates, while the subscription services that offer same products or services to all consumers recorded 13 percent of subscription renewal rate.[8] This result is testifying how a good curation can be an effective strategy to keep consumers from leaving the streaming service.

Lastly, service providers should deal with separation with a cool attitude. You can keep beautiful memories only when you let your ex go on a good note. Having complicated subscription cancellation policies or making it difficult to cancel a contract only hurts the brand image. Customers can come back any time only when they are allowed to leave any time. Similarly, service providers will also need to consider how to welcome customers when they return. Service providers should be able to convey the message that they have never forgotten about these returning customers and have been waiting for them instead of treating these returning customers as new customers.

The streaming market is expected to grow even faster in the future. According to Zuora, a company that mentioned the subscription economy for the first time, subscription-based industries are recording eight times the sales increase of the Standard & Poor's 500 companies, and five times the sales increase of U.S. retailers.[9] Because streaming services operate in the form of membership and subscription, they can become a reliable profit-generating model for businesses.

In Korea, companies specializing in rentals are also growing into powerful players. Recently, Coway코웨이 jumped to the second in the rank in about eight years since it launched a mattress rental service in 2011. This is a good example that shows how streaming has become the wind of change not just from the consumers' perspective, but also from the companies' perspective.

In 2020, customers who enjoy a streaming lifestyle will be offered more diverse and enriching services.

Technology for Hyper-Personalization

Data-driven personalization

A technology that understands each consumer's situation and the context in real-time, predicts their needs, and provides services and products is called hyper-personalization technology. Hyper-personalization technology develops individual profiles for each customer based on big data analyses. These profiles can then be used for a variety of purposes including providing relevant content and making recommendations. Important characteristics of this technology are to specify people's situations and to accommodate them more closely. The essence of this technology lies in how closely companies can accommodate the characteristics of their customers. Hyper-personalization technology will make intimate interactions between businesses and consumers possible, depending on how much consumer data businesses have and how meticulously they analyze the data in the entire manufacturing process of products and services.

Amazon is known for their goals to segment its customers scaled at 0.1 of a person. One customer in the digital world is not one person. To achieve accurate personalization reflecting various characteristics of one person, companies need to collect all analyzable data about their customers (1) at the point of contact, (2) analyze the data through AI algorithms, and (3) communicate with customers through diverse media channels. Ultimately, the goal of hyper-personalization technology is to predict the unique needs of customers and to provide services and products accordingly. However, from the perspective of customers, it is unpleasant and even unnerving that companies have detailed information about us. Thus, insightful government policies are needed to balance personal information protection, industry promotion, and consumer convenience. Optimistically, new knowledge and positive discourses will soon come in a hyper-personalized industry which will make this technology to emerge and flourish in 2020.

*C*ustomer A goes to a store to buy new shoes. The shoe store already knows exactly what brand he clicked the "like" button on last night on Instagram. As soon as he enters, his cell phone buzzes and he finds a discount code of the brand he liked last night texted to him. While he is looking around the store, digital signs keep guiding him to the corner where the style of shoes he is interested in is displayed. It is as if arrows are leading his steps just like in Alice in Wonderland. When he gets close to a pair of shoes and ponders if he wants to buy the pair or not, a special discount event pops up on his phone. When he examines another pair of shoes, a sales staff member comes to him with all the information he needs. He can buy a pair of shoes he wants at a customized price without haggling.

After work, Customer B returns home, lies in bed, and starts mobile shopping. As soon as she finds a pair of shoes that she loves, she impulsively presses the purchase button. At that moment, a warning alarm goes off, and a monthly salary management app kicks off and recommends another pair of shoes that is within her budget.

These are situations that could happen sooner than you think, because companies today are gearing up to become capable of responding to the rapidly changing consumption trend. A little frightening as they may be, these situations are becoming reality as fast as the speed of data accumulated in the digital world. While many companies are having difficulty managing brand reputation and maintaining brand identity because trends are changing so fast, personalized services that cater to consumers' tastes are becoming tools to fine-tune their relationships with consumers. Consumers are also embracing the trend of personalization. According to a survey by *Forbes*, 86 percent of consumers answered that personalized services had a certain impact on their purchases, and 25 percent of them also answered that personalization had a "significant impact" on their purchasing decisions.[1]

The future of personalization depends on how precisely businesses can understand their individual customers through customer data and computer algorithms. With the evolution of social medial and digital channels, businesses now have many more opportunities to collect data about their customers. In the past, "personalization" was achieved by integrating customers' personal information such as name, gender, and age with their transaction information such as their purchasing history. "Customer communication" meant sending customized messages to customers based on this type of information. But now, personalization is more than simply understanding customers' tastes and needs. It is evolving to a point where businesses can predict customers' future needs and communicate them in real time.

Amazon founder Jeff Bezos is known for his obsessive attention to the customer experience. His first strategy of customer experience is to respond to the instincts all customers have as a human being. The second is to resolve problems and stress resulting from the evolution of technology, and the third is to use Big Data and AI to implement one-on-one real time marketing with recommendations personalized to each user. The final strategy is to make customers forget they are making commercial transactions. It is about making customers feel that they are getting what they need, instead of "consuming a product."[2] Google also takes user variability as their priority from the start. In other words, the company starts from the recognition that a customer is not the same today as yesterday. Based on this awareness, the company is realizing the personalization of customers throughout their purchasing journey from visiting websites to searching and recommending products.

A technology that understands each consumer's situation and context in real time, predicts their needs, and provides services and products accordingly is called hyper-personalization technology(HPT hereinafter). HPT develops individual profiles for each customer based on big data analyses. These profiles can then be used for a variety of purposes including providing relevant content and making recommendations. Important characteristics of this technology are to specify people's situations and to accommodate them more closely. The essence of this technology lies in how closely companies can accommodate the idiosyncrasies of their customers. Competitiveness in hyper-personalization depends on how much consumer data businesses have and how meticulously they analyze the data in the entire manufacturing process of products and services. Needless to say, it is technological advances that have made such intimate interactions with consumers possible. Let us first take a look at the stages of the relevant technological advances.

Three Stages of Hyper-Personalization Technology

Stage 1: Data from Everywhere

Technologies that sound only from science fictions could become reality thanks to the enormous amount of "data" that is generated and collected from various places through sensors. Data is collected from GPS, Wi-Fi, motion sensors, SMS, calendars and many other sources to analyze users' lifestyle patterns and recommend necessary information based on the results of the analysis. Various data types are necessary to predict consumers' simple behaviors and to find hidden patterns identify consumers' true intentions behind their behavioral patterns. All data types such as location data, purchase history, demographics, data collected from IoT devices, smart-watch data and mobile device data, are the basic units of analysis. In addition, user-generated data from reviews on social media are also important factors. Data collected from every touch point throughout a consumer's purchasing journey tells all interactions that took place between businesses and consumers and helps businesses to meet the expectations of their customers who have grown accustomed to personalization.

Recently, the Beijing-based transportation company Didi Chuxing was put in hot water over a criminal case between its driver and passenger. This sparked controversy over passenger safety, to which DiDi Chuxing responded by taking drastic measures to restore consumer confidence and improve internal work efficiency. One of the actions it took was developing a driver assignment system based on big data. Based on 7 years of data on 30 million cars a day, the company analyzed drivers' driving habits and developed a system that could select a driver who is the best fit for a given passenger.

It is a time to shift from the post-industrial revolution mass production system and even the following small quantity batch production system to a production system that caters to all needs of individual customers. If you want to apply the HPT to business, even the small quantity batch production system cannot fully meet the demands of individual customers. HPT moves along with changes in production methods, such as modulization of production lines that can be modified to meet the diversifying demands of individual customers. This change is expected to happen along with the micro-modularization methods which maximize the variability of product production methods. These methods include producing parts at the minimum scale like small Lego blocks and assembling them to produce products that individual consumers demand and producing colors and shapes individual customers demand through variable production systems. When this trend progresses, uniformed products that are supplied to general consumers will no longer be able to sustain in the market.

Stage 2: Algorithm Analysis Through AI

Randomly collected vast amount of data does not really tell you anything by itself. The key is how to analyze it. Hyper-personalization through data analysis is made possible by machine learning and AI. AI is ultimately geared towards hyper-personalization. It is about applying algorithms and finding values that are optimized for users based on Big Data and their search history.

HPT begins with big data analyses on how much time each customer spends shopping online and what items each customer adds to their shopping cart or to their wish list.

Personalization can constantly change the process of designing customers' purchases by utilizing AI and real-time data. It can read the minds of customers more accurately if businesses take into consideration external variables and the context of the consumers' purchases, such as the consumer's age bracket, time, weather, and date in addition to hyper-personalization. Understanding of AI, Internet of Things, 5G, virtual reality, and AR is essential in order to read our future trends and technologies and realize hyper-personalization. The level of the interaction between customers and businesses will improve if businesses can secure more and detailed data – such as additional information about more relative content, products, and services – and thoroughly analyze it with more advanced algorithms to apply the results to each user.

Stage 3: Interactive Communication Through Diverse Media Channels

Even if a company has accumulated data and develops an AI system that analyzes it, the company cannot fully utilize this technology unless the company has a means to communicate with its customers. In the past, companies unilaterally provided information about their products and collected specific information from their consumers. Now, however, development in media technology has made it easier for companies and consumers to communicate with each other through comments on social media or various customer-generated content. More efficient communication becomes possible as the focus of targeting strategies shifts from the unspecified general public to more segmented consumers.

Interactive communication is a powerful touch point that allows businesses to have deeper understanding of their customers and to approach their customers more intimately. The Chinese company, Tencent believes that increased interactive communication is an important condition for a winning business. Tencent argues that increased use of communication apps and an increased number of customer reach points(CRP) imply increased commitment of a company to its customers, and this will become a key factor in determining which companies win or lose in the market. Tencent has a wide range of CRPs including Internet portals, messenger service QQ and mobile messenger WeChat. In addition, its mobile payment service WeChat Pay is one of the two leading simple payment services along with Alipay in China. Almost all startup services – such as renting bicycles(Mobike), calling taxis(DiDi Chuxing), making appointments with doctors, and paying utility bills – are connected to WeChat Pay. The more CRPs businesses have through diverse media channels and platforms, the more clearly businesses can draw portraits of their customers.

The Direction of HPT: Context-oriented Understanding of Consumer Needs

Reading Consumer Context

The application of HPT starts with a business under standing the context of its customers. For example, if someone is using a taxi app repeatedly for a ride home late at night, the app can learn the user's pattern of calling for a taxi after working a night shift and predict when the user is likely to request a ride again. If the service provider opens the app on the user's phone just when the user might need a ride home, the user can save time by not having to open an app and request a taxi.

HPT uses machine learning based on Big Data to find patterns and treat people as more segmented individuals. To support this process, an accurate understanding of customer situations is essential. In addition, from the consumers' point of view, the advantage is that they can purchase exactly what they need and from the suppliers' perspective, the advantage of this accurate delivery of service is that they can ensure greater customer satisfaction, brand loyalty of customers, and cut unnecessary marketing costs.

According to the results of studies by Microsoft, the time online users pay attention to online content items is getting shorter.[3] Their studies show that consumers usually concentrate on a content item for about eight seconds.

That means consumers prefer shorter content over long content, but they spend an average of three hours a day searching for purchase-related information and web surfing.[4] Supported by these study results, Amazon opened a door to personalized marketing strategies with such innovative measures as recommending products to customers based on their past browsing and purchasing history so that customers can buy what they need with just one click of a button.

Perfect Matches with Consumers

Based on behavioral economics and hyper-personalization technologies, Shinhan Card신한카드 has been responding to each consumer's needs more intimately with benefits that are tailored to their personal situations. For example, the correlation between a particular customer's ice cream preference and supermarket consumption rate is analyzed, and then the consideration of weather conditions such as a heat wave is added to the analysis results, so that the supermarket can send that particular customer timely discount coupons for a certain product. With this approach, the card company has reportedly recorded a 2~4 times higher response rate than when they sent out the same messages to unspecified multiple customers.

This example shows the necessity to provide customers with optimal personalized benefits at just the right time by upgrading the conventional benefit recommendation service to higher level and reflecting the customers' TPO (time, place, and occasion). While in the past, benefits were offered on a monthly or daily basis, but now, weather and the commercial zone information on current location of customers are reflected on the system in real time, so that businesses can provide personalized benefits depending on their situations. Supported by these study results, the card company launched Shinhan Deep Making card which allows customers to pick benefits for themselves and Shinhan Card Deep Taking card which provides personalized services in five areas the customers use most frequently.

Boston Consulting Group predicts that companies' profits will increase by at least 6~10 percent through the implementation of personalization technology.[5] The strategy of sending personalized messages is the first step toward reading consumer's context and providing personalized services. The next step is to segment consumers into different groups based on the data about them, and to deliver messages in the form with contents that is tailored for each group. Currently, 90 percent of companies are at this stage. The next step is the emergence of HPT that can understand consumers' behaviors and provide products and services tailored to them by taking a closer look at consumer data. Personalized information should be made deliverable through channels and messages that are most approachable for them, such as magazine articles, television,

Facebook, Instagram, and so on. Ultimately, personalized recommendation and HPT will evolve to the point where customers have their purchases anticipated by companies even before they realize it themselves.

Values that Hyper-Personalization Pursues: the Three "A"s

What should we give heed to for the realization of hyper-personalization? Let's take a look at this with three "A"s as the values that hyper-personalization should pursue.

1. Awareness of Users

The first value that HPT should pursue is to identify individual consumers' situations. The first stage of hyper-personalization is to find out where consumers are, doing what, and in what context.

One good example is the Starbucks mobile "ready" push notification, which notifies consumers that their orders are ready without using a bell. Another example is smart medicine bottles with a built-in alarm that goes off when it is time for the user to take a dose. In this case, the medicine bottle is linked with a mobile app so that the alarm goes off when it is time to take the medicine, and when the user responds to the alarm, the bottle opens automatically so that the user can take the medicine out. It has an additional feature that allows users to check the bottle open-and-closing history, making it an essential service for certain groups of users.

There is a new type of media that is under the direct control of a marketer, such as app push, messaging-based media, and email. This type of media is called "owned media." People might think that when sending a traditional-type message through an owned media, they can reach the highest number of people if they send the message to as many people as possible. But if you keep sending messages to an unspecified random group of people, those messages are likely to go to the "spam" box. Therefore, it is important to send messages tailored to individual customers at the most appropriate time. To do this, a business needs to gather data on customer reaction to each message. Getting recognized by customers is the first step in applying HPT.

Connecting lighting systems to the IoT at home is another good example of this technology bringing convenience in various situations. The lighting system can be programmed to trigger a warning light when there is an intruder or turn on a light when a child is coming too close to a stove or stairway so that parents can be aware of it. The lighting can also be programmed to blink to let elderly household members know it's time to take medicine. In addition, lights with wireless access network equipment can track how much energy household appliances are consuming, ultimately allowing light bulb manufacturers to make energy saving suggestions to homeowners and electric companies. These are some of the examples that show how the IoT technology helps make hyper-personalization possible by identifying unique situations of individual consumers.

2. Assistance to Users

Second, once you understand the situations or contexts of the consumers, then you can go for the technologies that help businesses to be "together" with their consumers in those situations. Some good examples of these technologies include chatbot, AI speakers, and a smart home system. Chatbot is already taking a big part in handling customer service, and with the introduction of HPT, it is evolving to the point where it can listen to customers' inquiries and requests in further detail.

For example, the music streaming service Spotify offers Your Daily Drive, which provides subscribers with a personalized playlist of their favorite songs, podcasts, and relevant news updates that they can enjoy during their daily drive to work. The playlist is curated based on data drawn from the music or podcast channels one has been listening to behind the wheel. If a person has been listening to a specific podcast channel while driving, that person will be offered a playlist that includes updates from that podcast channel. The person does not have to visit the podcast channel separately any more. Spotify also developed a music selection service called Weekly Discovery, which is about providing lists of music sources to each of over 70 million subscribers. Spotify subscribers can listen to the music that suits their taste and occasions, and some people even claim that "Spotify knows what music I like better than I do." The secret that made Spotify the leader in the fiercely competitive music source market is a recommendation algorithm that can accurately understand the users' taste in music.

AI speakers are another good example of technology that promises convenience to users. The market research firm Strategy Analytics announced that as of the second quarter of 2019, 30 million AI speakers had been sold globally, which marks a 96 percent increase from the same period a year earlier. The domestic AI speaker market is also growing rapidly. According to the Ministry of Science, Information and Communication, the cumulative sales of AI speakers recorded 4.12 million units in the first half of 2019, which is more than double from the previous year when 2 million AI speakers were sold.[6] Recently, Korean companies have launched a voice recognition AI service, which allows you to make a phone call to somebody just by speaking the name to the device, and the technology has advanced to the point where you just enter a few words to find the movie that you would like. All the conversations you have with the devices are saved in the Cloud so that they can be recycled by being analyzed and processed into Big Data, which in turn makes AI learn more about you and develop new and better services for you.

Anticipating User Behavior

In addition to awareness and assist, the final value pursued by HPT is anticipation of customers' next moves.

Most online retailers try to accurately anticipate what consumers will demand. Amazon is the unrivaled leader in this area. Amazon anticipates consumer demands by proactively utilizing cost-saving machine learning. The company is investing in the business service called "anticipated delivery', which is about predicting the possibility of customers ordering certain products based on the analysis of all types of data, such as the purchasing history, products added to their carts, products that they haven't purchased yet, and even the movement of the customers' cursors. Supported by this technology, Amazon was able to cut the cost of two-day usual shipping to the cost of standard shipping, which is a saving of 66 percent, and now send products to the logistics hubs that are closest to each customer's address. By the time customers place an order, the product is already waiting for the order at the nearest logistics base. This was how Amazon was able to cut down both shipping cost and delivery time. Supported by the data on book purchasing for the past 20 years, Amazon is practicing taste anticipation marketing on all products including DVDs and special miniatures, not to mention introducing newly released books that each customer might like.

The online video service provider (OTT) Netflix is another company that succeeded in anticipating consumers' tastes through HPT. Netflix is satisfying each subscribing viewer's demand for videos by developing a variety of programs and algorithms that accurately understand their tastes. Netflix sends a weekly email or text message to each subscriber, telling them that new videos that they might like have been just released. This approach of providing highly detailed hyper-personalized services to individual subscribers in the target group has been the foundation of the company's success.

Implications

"Amazon segments customers on a scale of 0.1 persons."

This is what Andreas Weigend said about Amazon in his book, *Data for the People: How to Make Our Post-Privacy Economy Work for You*. This statement is a good description of the direction of HPT which needs to reflect each consumer's constantly changing needs in a timely manner. With the development of HPT, companies will be able to identify more than just the customer within a person; they will find "numerous invisible consumers within a person." Since the technology is capable of observing each customer from multiple angles, it allows companies to save time and resources, not to mention adding diverse customer experiences. It can also improve consumers' quality of life with its ability to give recommendations to each customer based on the intimate communications between customers and businesses. Furthermore, customers' quality of life will be improved through the ability to understand each customer's taste and anticipate what they would order.[8] But however rosy its prospects may be, we need to look at its dark shadows as well.

Martin Heidegger in the 1950s observed that "the wave of technological revolution will distract us and blind us until certain ideas will be accepted and implemented as if they were the only way to think." As hyper-personalization became possible through the realization of technologies including data collection and algorithm analysis, Heidegger's prediction is being realized in the 21st century. As explained in the keyword "Multi Persona" part of this book, it is also problematic that hyper-personalization curation is likely to be shaped by companies instead of being used to reflect the taste of each consumer. This problem can escalate when

Hyper-personalization technology develops individual profiles for each customer based on big data analyses. Important characteristics of this technology are to specify people's situations and to accommodate them more closely.

users are unsure about their own tastes.

In fact, the global use of data collection and AI utilization are dominated by a small number of U.S. and Chinese power-user companies known as GAFA (Google, Amazon, Facebook, Apple) and BATH (Baidu, Alibaba, Tencent, and Huawei). Companies that dominate the market can observe consumers more closely and accumulate more data. Naturally, they have better understanding of consumers and create better algorithms, thereby creating a virtuous cycle (positively feedback) and the strong become the stronger. It is like the logic of the rich get richer and the poor get poorer is applied to data and technology areas, and data is utilized by those companies as a form of power to look down on the market like Almighty God. They can penetrate deeper into people's lives and secure more accurate information than they have now, consequently consolidating their current status. This chain of consequences shows how privacy issues and market economy logic are moving hand in hand together. Ultimately, concerns over the relationship between Big Data and privacy are expected to grow.

It will not be too long before the manufacturing and distribution industries are dominated by the ones that secure all types of necessary data and use algorithm analysis to occupy all platforms that are subject to hyper-personalization. Our purchase history can be bought and sold among companies that want to share them when you mindlessly click on the privacy sharing policy. Companies are striving to get their hands on the purchasing histories of consumers in order to survive in the market. That is the reason credit cards and financial companies are frequently experiencing breaches of their customers' personal information. Debates over pros and cons over HPT will heat up when it clashes with social values, making people wonder what should come first, freedom or control, possession or sharing, opening or closing. It is also time for the government to come up with insightful plans to balance the protection of personal information, fostering industries, and consumer convenience.

From the perspective of customers, it is unpleasant and even unnerving that companies have detailed information about them, because this could mean the Big Brother society described in George Orwell's book *1984* becomes a reality. Despite many concerns, however, competition among companies to survive in the market economy will further fuel the race for hyper-personalization through Big Data and AI. Now, technology knows about us better than we do about ourselves.

You're with Us

'Fansumer'

Consumers do not find it satisfactory simply by purchasing one option from a list of alternatives. They now have a desire to personally participate in the investment and manufacturing process of developing products, brands, and stars. This new type of consumer who takes part in the entire life cycle of a product, and who actively supports and purchases a product with the pride of "having raised it personally," while at the same time meddling in and exercising their control over it, is termed a "fansumer." These fansumers believe that big and small changes are driven by themselves, and this can be called the "by-me" syndrome.

The paradigm of consumption has shifted from ownership to experience. And the paradigm is now again shifting from experience to "engagement." This "engagement fever" is affecting all processes of the market including selecting, growing, developing, producing, distributing, and marketing products as well as supporting and criticizing them. The fansumers' influence is continuously expanding. Some fansumers participate in crowd-funding to invest in the businesses that they like and whose causes they agree with. Others become "supporters" to enthusiastically participate in development, merchandising, and marketing activities. Fansumers in the entertainment business even get involved in the policies of entertainment agencies, including decisions about which entertainers should be debuted. Lately, as influencers — the social media equivalent of celebrities are — becoming a target of fansumers, influencers are also experiencing both support and criticism from their fans. The growth of fansumers is not just a passing trend. This growth is a necessary consequence of the self-efficacy of millennials and Generation X who are becoming the driving force of a market with solid industrial and technological foundations. Fansumers should be made into assets. Without fansumers, there is no growth in entertainment, marketing, or any other business, not even in politics.

The word "fan" is said to have originated from the word "fanatic" and was shortened to "fan" to make it easier to pronounce. The suffix word "dom" was added to it, and that's how the word "fandom" came about. Originally, the word "fandom" referred to "some individual or group of people who demonstrate enthusiasm for something or someone, particularly a celebrity," but recently, the meaning has expanded to include the whole range of activities that people do to prove their fandom, such as purchasing certain products. Now, fandom is evolving again into the "fansumer." Fansumers are consumers whose fandom is more committed and proactive to the point where they will not only love the objects of their admiration and purchase those object-related products. Fansumers will also have direct interactions with them by developing events and projects, investing in them, and even playing the role of keeping them in check. The rise of fansumers has a lot to do with the young generation – the "fair players" with a high level of efficacy, as explained in the "fair play" part of this book – taking part in the entire manufacturing process.

Fansumers are engaged in a wide range of activities. They are engaged in supporting entertainers to make them stars, investing in startups with promising idea products, taking part in the product development process, participating in marketing activities as supporters, and sometimes they don't hesitate to criticize and even reprimand entertainers or influencers. The driving force behind these fansumer activities is their pride in "having contributed to their success." This can be defined as "by-me syndrome" because it is all about their sense of efficacy that tells them it was made "by me."

The consumption paradigm that shifted from ownership to experience is now evolving from experience to engagement. The enthusiasm for this engagement is now spreading throughout the markets from choosing and raising a star, product idea and its production, distribution and marketing, and supporting and criticizing. Having been personally engaged in the entire life cycle of a product, the consumers have pride in their contribution to the birth of a product, and this pride encourages them to exercise their power to check and interfere. As their support, purchasing, and methods of investment are expanding to a point we have never seen before, the phenomenon is creating some negative side effects as well. Now, let's take a look at the various side effects of the "by-me syndrome" created by these proactive fansumers.

Various Aspects of the By-me Syndrome

1. Crowdfunding : An Alliance Between Fandom and Investment

Now, investment is not just for financial institutions or professional investors. Thanks to crowdfunding, anyone can do it with a small amount of money if they are interested. Crowdfunding refers to the way companies are financed through investments from multiple individual investors, and its total amount recorded nearly 22.5 billion won as of the first half of 2019. The amount invested in those six months is already 70 percent of the 30.3 billion won raised in 2018.[1]

Crowdfunding is a new investment method that satisfies both a cause and practical interest, because it makes investors feel proud of financially supporting a business item that they are interested in or has a great cause, while they can expect a certain amount of return on their investment, not to mention various forms of compensation. Like a modern-day equivalent to the ancient communal sharing of labor, the makers pitch their ideas to receive investment funds, while the people who want that idea to become a commercial success make their investments in those projects. The action of funding for the creation of a product that has never been made, or a product that does not exist in reality yet, can also bring the pleasure of becoming a shareholder. It doesn't matter if they are just small shareholders, because in crowdfunding, everyone is just a small shareholder.

Crowdfunding is largely divided into securities, sponsorship and donation types. Securities type refers to crowdfunding where investors become a shareholder or creditor of a company in exchange for their investment, and they can get profit in the form of return. It literally is a form of financial investment in anticipation of investment returns. From the perspective of a company, it serves as useful financing for small and medium-sized companies and startups because it is less burdensome than loans, which require payments of interest on top of the principal. On the other hand, the sponsorship type is about multiple sponsors providing funds for a given project and getting certain forms of return other than financial gain. It is mainly used in performance, music, film, education, and environment projects. Lastly, this donation type is similar to the sponsorship type, but in this case, they support a project purely for the purpose of supporting it without expecting any reward in return.

The centerpiece of crowdfunding certainly is the sponsorship type that promises a rewarding sense of participation as well as actual rewards, particularly in the form of the product that investors are sponsoring. That is the reason it is called "reward-based crowdfunding". In the case of reward-based and donation-based crowdfunding, makers have to compensate investors with a reward when the product or service becomes available. Consumer investors can expect to get not just a return on their investment, but they can also feel proud of themselves, because they will become the first to use a product or service that is introduced to the world for the first time. It is a characteristic of the millennial generation to pursue advance experiences with trust as collateral. That is the reason the millennial generation is interested in the reward-based crowdfunding.

Crowdfunding started with the first-generation of American startups such as Kickstarter and Indigo, and they were followed by many other platforms such as Tumblbug, Goodfunding and Incujector, all of which are growing popular among fansumers who wish to participate in financial support campaigns. In Korea, a crowdfunding platform, Wadiz와디즈, is growing rapidly with the number of projects jumping to 4,634 as of September 2019 from just 501 in 2015. The platform has grown into a service that helps over 400 companies per month to get the funds while being a steppingstone for new startup brands. Tumblbug텀블벅, a platform specializing in reward-based crowdfunding, also recorded 5,089 funding projects in 2018, and the industry predicts that the platform will have no problem in recording 7,000 funding projects by the end of 2019. This is how fansumers surf diverse platforms to enjoy new and sound ways of consumption, while making investments and getting rewards.

There are several advantages of crowdfunding that attract people's interest, including relatively reasonably priced rewards because it is done in the form of a direct transaction through an online network. It also has better promotional effects for makers because of the high level of loyalty from consumers who have participated in the crowdfunding. There is a growing popularity of funding platforms that turn investment into a hobby. It is because investors who made an investment as a hobby can sometimes receive significant returns. One successful example is the Japanese animation movie *Your Name Is*. The Korean company Media Castle turned to crowdfunding to come up with the 150 million won that they needed to release the Japanese movie in Korean theaters in the form of a securities type crowdfunding, in which additional interests could be expected depending on how well the movie did in Korea. The movie ended up recording 3.76 million box office ticket sales and the investors received an additional return of 70 percent (APR) on top of the basic return of 10 percent (APR), making the movie one of the most successful cases of crowdfunding.

The consumers' financial support of the makers and exercising their due rights as investors is a very desirable form of consumer culture. But there is something that shouldn't be overlooked: the duality of sponsorship. Investment fuels expectations, and while waiting, those expectations grow even bigger. It should be noted that there is always a risk of disappointing fansumers who may become angry at the makers if they receive rewards that are not what they'd expected.

2. Futuristic Form of a Communal Sharing of Labor: Participation in the Development Process and Support Activity

Netflix's drama series *Black Mirror Bandersnatch* has built fandom with innovative interactive content that allowed viewers to participate and change the story line and even the ending. There are five officially recognized endings, and there are over ten unofficial endings, all of which testify to the enthusiastic participation of the drama's fansumers.[2] Viewers and subscribers are not only sending their support and kudos to movies and dramas, but they are also getting directly involved in their production process as well, such as casting. However, companies and brands seem to be more than happy to see these consumers who are overstepping their boundaries as consumers. It is because fansumer-utilizing fandom marketing can create a promotional effect as well as a lock-in effect that improves their loyalty to the brand. Companies allow their interference in return for their purchasing and promotional efforts afterward. In this sense, it can be understood as a futuristic equivalent of the communal sharing of labor in old days.

The performance theater industry is also actively engaged in attracting fansumers. The impromptu murder investigation play *Murder Mystery* introduced an interesting new format in which a play is improvised based on ideas that the audience suggests such as the background of a murder, murder weapon, killer, and victim. Another theater play *Sheer Madness* tells of a murder that took place in a beauty salon which allows the audience to become the witness and participate in the interrogation of suspects. The audience can ask questions during the play, and the victim is confirmed by the vote of the audience after interrogation is over. Their strategy of creating rapport with the participation of the audience and enhancing their loyalty by encouraging their further engagement is a good example of utilizing fansumers' participation and cheering traits.

Fansumers propose, plan and create products that are completely new, but they also revive products that have been retired as well. One example is Coca-Cola's "Surge Movement" for the return of the Surge soda that was discontinued in 2003. The product's hard-core fansumers raised $3,837 to put up a billboard in front of Coca-Cola's headquarters and eventually got the company to re-release it after their revival campaign. In Korea, snacks that had been discontinued years ago, such as Chitos White, Sun Chip, and Chicken Pop, have been re-released as well. Now, fansumers are more than just consumers. They are playing a role of partners for companies by using their influence in the decision-making process of companies, consequently reviving products that had been long gone from the market.

Fansumers are also dynamic supporters of companies. Xiaomi of China is a company that realized the importance of fansumers before others did. Xiaomi is practicing a strategy to use the company's fanatic fandom, Mifan to increase consumer loyalty to their products. Mifan consumers review all the products and content items Xiaomi produces, but they don't receive any payment from Xiaomi in return. They buy products made by Xiaomi and invest their efforts to promote Xiaomi to prove their support for Xiaomi's corporate activities. When Xiaomi created its own operating system called MIUI for smartphone users, it received such rave feedback that their fansumers have been posting over 200,000 messages and more than 100 million comments every day. One can say that Mifan is the best fandom marketing that would make any company jealous.

3. Justified Interference Beyond Fandom: Fansumers in Entertainment Industry

The activities of fansumers are most noticeable in the entertainment industry, where passionate fans emerged as industry movers and shakers for the first time. Some of the most extraordinary examples can be found in the idol industry that is at the top of all entertainment businesses. The evolution to "star-nurturing type fandom" with purchasing power gave celeb fans a sense of entitlement beyond their rights. Hard-core fansumers go one step further from just raising stars and speaking up to have their voices heard loud and clear. It is like the fans are claiming to be entitled to speak up because they have been raising and supporting those celebs.

SM Entertainment had a bout of trouble over the idol group EXO's performance in Japan. It was because their touring schedule included a performance in a venue located in Miyagi Prefecture, a region close to the site of the 2011 Fukushima nuclear accident and importing fisheries from that region is banned by the Korean government. Some members of EXO's fan clubs found out about this and protested against the group's tour to Japan, categorically claiming, "Booking a tour schedule at the cost of the members' health shows how the agent of the idol group considers them only as their property."[3]

Then came the incident involving the idol selection audition program *Produce 101*, whose production crew were charged for having rigged the selection process when 260 fans of the losers reported the broadcasting and production companies to the authorities. The prosecution launched an investigation into the case, and fans formed a fictional idol group with losers as its members, named the group BY9 (Be

Your 9), created a logo for the group, and launched their own promotional campaign after collecting 100 million won in contributions. When the idols that they were supporting failed in the audition, they raised the money to give them a chance to make a debut on their own. These examples testify to the commitment of fansumers that is growing more daring and aggressive.

Shin Yoon-hee, the author of *Fandom 3.0*, summed up today's idol fandom as a trading and managing fandom of love, as opposed to the past "groupies" who were only supporting their idols by admiring and loving them. When the winner from Produce 101, Kang Daniel, released a solo album, it recorded more than 460,000 sales by his fans, and some of his fans donated 1,210,725 (a combination of Kang Daniel's birthday, December 10, and the date of his comeback on July 25) won to the Korea Childhood Leukemia Foundation to build a good image to him.

However, fansumers are not there as blindfolded givers. They usually shower their idols with unlimited love and support, but when their idols do something wrong, they can be the coldest-hearted criticizers. When the quality of Kang Daniel's solo album fell short of their expectations, his fans started criticizing him mercilessly, while analyzing the reasons for the poor quality, and some fansumers left the fan club claiming that he had no hope for improvement. They recognize themselves as producers and publicists instead of being just ordinary fans, and they can turn their backs decisively after criticizing them just as much as they'd supported them when their idols fail to meet their high expectations on them..

4. Pros and Cons Over Influencers

The relationship between fans and fansumers is also evident in their relationships with influencers, who are considered the social media equivalent of entertainers. Influencers are also a group of entertainers who are monetizing on the fandom that they build and maintain. Consumers actually react to and enjoy watching what these influencers eat, carry, and do. But when these influencers are found to have been deceiving and ignoring their followers, their fansumers don't hesitate to reprimand them.

Companies that have been trying hard to recruit influencers are now channeling their resources to growing their own "home-grown" influencers. Kia Motors Corp., the first car maker to launch a professional creator training program, pays a total of 20 million won for the activities of their creators, while Hanwha Group, a company that runs an internship program for travel content producers, is also supporting their three-day domestic trips and five-day overseas trips as a part of their endeavor to produce their own influencers. Companies are striving to foster their own influencers because the content items created from the perspective of an influencer – who is also an ordinary consumer – works much better than those made from the perspective of the companies, and their support for these influencers can also bring them well-organized fansumer groups as a bonus. The company-sponsored influencers are important fansumers for the companies, and since these influencers' followers are their fansumers as well, it makes it easier to build a strong affectionate relationship with them, too.

Factors and Background of the Growth in Fansumers

The growth of fansumers is not just a fad. It can be considered as the inevitable consequence of the complex impact of the generational characteristics of the millennials and generation Z, who have become the main axis of economy at a time when industrial and technological foundations are well established.

First of all, the rapidly growing idol industry is one of the main backgrounds behind the phenomenon. The so-called "fun-loving generation X" who had been the main players during the golden days of Korean pop culture is spearheading the nurturing-type of fandom culture. Fans in their 30s and 40s, who are financially stable and in a similar as group as the idols' aunts and uncles, are moving those idols with more organized and significantly scaled support.

These fans would cancel even a confirmed concert for the sake of protecting their star idols struggling with a packed schedule, and they made a feminism movie that didn't seem likely to reach the break-even point eventually become a box office success by using such methods as repeatedly going to movie theaters to watch it or "sending souls (buying tickets to support the success of the movie but too busy to go to watch the movie physically). Having a strong sense of solidarity, these fan clubs participate in projects with socially significant causes, and they are also active in making donations. Their engagements are not restricted only to supporting entertainers or cultural products, and they are naturally connecting to the participation and investment in other industries and influencers.

Second, there is the change in the mobile media environment as a technical foundation. Incubated on social media, the general public builds a relationship with a brand or company, and further, with society, while thinking and acting through engagement.

Engagement, which can be explained as "customer participation" or even "customer loyalty" is an indicator of the influence or the sense of intimacy consumers feel about a certain brand. It manifests in the form of reactions that cause an action, such as hitting the "like" button on social media, sharing such as a regram or retweet, and comments. It means the development of mobile technology is fueling the growth of the fansumer population. But no matter how an industry is prospering and how much technology is there to support them, trends will be hard to form without a group of consumers who actively use them.

The third background is the characteristics of the millennial generation, who enjoy justifiable consumption motivated by a good cause. Some of the characteristics of the millennial consumers include that they want socially significant consumption, and they join forces to take action for self-purification and cleaning-up. They pursue taste consumption, but taste does not take priority over cause. Individually they are weak, but together, they have momentum. Millennials frequently band and disband to speak up about their beliefs. They enjoy salon culture with their taste as the medium, or they participate in classes to share their interest and learn things together. They eagerly cast their votes in campaigns with a good cause, and they preach to others about what they believe in and urge them to join their cause. These are the sides of the millennials who practice justified consumption and take action autonomously.

The movement by fansumer starts with "joining." The fansumers' solidarity power comes from a little sense of belonging. On top of this, millennials have such characteristics as spontaneity, professionalism and information collecting skills, all of which helped them evolve into smart consumers. In the past, boycotting products from companies that are caught doing something immoral was the most powerful collective activity that consumers could join in. However, when the idol industry started growing, it was the average viewers who held the key to victory or defeat in the ever-growing competition among idol groups. Consumers began to see how the choices made by ordinary individuals like themselves contribute to the birth of super stars, and that made them grow powerful. Consumers have exerted their influence through the act of "joining" and they have come to believe that their small act of joining can help change the world. The power of collective intelligence and the spreading sense of solidarity enhances their self-efficacy, pushing fansumers to become more and more involved in sponsorship activities.

Implications

Whether you own a sustainable fandom or not has become the determinant of corporate competitiveness. From the perspective of companies, the spontaneity of fansumers is a great asset in business management.

Companies need elaborate loyalty programs to build and

The paradigm of consumption has shifted from ownership to experience, and the paradigm is now again shifting from experience to "engagement." Without fansumers, there is no growth in entertainment, marketing, or any other business, not even in politics.

maintain fandom so that they can make customers their supporters and partners instead of just selling products to them. If well managed, initiatives that are meant to promote customer engagements – such as subscription, making comments, sharing posts, visiting websites, and purchasing products – can offer opportunities for companies to build data necessary for hyper-personalization. Now, fansumers are becoming a corporate asset in many ways.

Crowdfunding is a main stage for fansumers where possibilities are bought and sold, because it is where brand new ideas are presented and financed to be realized through interactive communication between developers and crowd sponsors. That's the reason a growing number of companies are beginning to use crowdfunding as a channel for predicting consumer demand. By listening to the opinions of the customers who participated in a crowdfunding project, companies can reflect their opinions to improve their product, not to mention enjoying a positive marketing effect. Since it costs less than other distribution platforms, companies can also cut distribution costs and consumer prices too.

A sound common sense in consumption should spread so that a culture of symbiosis can take root throughout society. Fansumers not being reluctant to chip in for public interest activities, they are attracted to the opportunities where they can get an intangible but fulfilling sense of reward. If you want to explain the interactive consumer-brand relationship that creates common interest in a more complex and comprehensive manner, you need a system that can measure the intensity and depth of consumer engagement.

Consumers also need to understand that sponsorship is different from group purchase. When you invest money in something, you are entitled to have a sense of ownership, but you also have to be willing to take responsibility in case of problems. In reality, an increasing number of people have participated in one after another bad projects that ended up losing money.

There is also an increasing number of cases in which companies raise funds successfully only to go bankrupt soon after. Recently, a system was introduced by a platform company to assign a law firm to mediate conflicts between companies and investors. Crowdfunding is certainly a promising field, but it is also an imperfect market that is in need of systems and relevant government policies.

Be it entertainment, marketing, politics, or any business, it is difficult to grow without fansumers. We need to create a virtuous circle structured to build a better world together by using the "by-me syndrome" of fansumers who are in a symbiotic relationship with these interests as the driving force. Now, "with customers" alone is not good enough. In the fansumer market that is moved "by the customers," companies need to reach out to consumers first for their passionate support and engagement.

Make or Break, Specialize or Die

Specialization

You have to specialize to survive. Assured satisfaction of a selected few has become more important than appealing to all customers. The development of online distribution has activated a long-tail economy. The overheated competition has made it difficult to notice differences between products. As consumer needs have grown extremely individualized, the standardized mass-market approach will not help businesses gain consumers. With all the fast-paced changes and ever-growing competition, companies can no longer depend on the "survival of the fittest" approach. They now have to evolve to incorporate "survival of the specialized" strategies.

Think of the glass shoe that perfectly fits only Cinderella. In order to create a market that precisely fits each — one and only — customer, companies need to carefully observe their target group, segment the group into more hyper-targeted groups, and come up with specialized strategies for each of them. Valid and detailed segmentation strategies are crucial for successful specialization. To achieve this, companies need to (1) sort out a target market based on customer characteristics like tweezers, (2) zoom in on one aspect of scattered customer needs like a microscope, (3) understand the characteristics of local commercial zones by drawing concentric circles like a compass, and (4) focus on the company's competitiveness like a fishing rod.

We are not simply in an economy of customer satisfaction; we are in an economy of customer hyper-satisfaction. Instead of trying to appeal to random mass, unspecified people who may or may not have interests in your company and products, it is more effective to exclusively focus on those few who show clear interests. The niche becomes the rich. Narrow down, cut down, and sharpen your edge. In 2020, there will be an abundance of hyper-precise specialization strategies augmented with agile methodologies, hyper-targeting, and micro-managing.

"Our target is a 32-year-old professional woman who owns a condo and likes to travel and exercise. We don't care about 33 years old or 31 years old."

This is the profile of target customers described by Chip Wilson, founder of Canadian yoga outfit brand, Lululemon, which is considered the sportswear equivalent of Chanel. This profile description of a super woman who has a professional career and works out wearing yoga pants that cost more than $100 clearly illustrates Lululemon's philosophy of painstakingly specific "targeting." It also shows Lululemon's philosophy of meticulous specialization. Lululemon is arguably the leader in "athleisure fashion", which refers to sportswear that can be worn like everyday clothes. Of course, women aged 31 or 33 can be their customers too, but Lululemon knows exactly who to target. It is quite possible that such a painstakingly elaborate micro-targeting strategy helped Lululemon rank fifth among sportswear brands in terms of revenue in 2018, which was a big jump from 11th in 2013.[1] This is a feat that clearly shows the power of specialization by focusing on a specific target group based on the company's strength.

In dart games, there is a rule about scoring. If you hit the red center, or Single Bull as it is called, you earn 50 points, but if you hit the general area (Singles), you only score from 1 to 20, even though singles are right next to the single bull. The center of the dartboard, such as the single bull, is called the bullseye, and depending on which part of the board you strike, the difference in score can be as high as 50. If we may use the previous success case as a dart game, Lululemon can be explained as having achieved outstanding success because it hit the target of the market right on the bullseye.

The success of a business depends on the creation of products and services that hit the bullseye, a point where the market needs and the business' capabilities crisscross. Focusing on this narrow but important area is called "targeting," and it is essential to make a more precise targeting possible. In a rapidly changing world where the needs of consumers are increasingly diversified, businesses are busy splitting, dividing, and focusing. Now, specialization is more than about differentiation; it has become a condition of survival. The survival of the specialized, which is a concept more evolved from the survival of the fittest, is a new prescription for corporate management that is essential to survive intensifying competition. Let's look at the types, background, cases and methodologies associated with the conditions for survival.

Specialization Strategies

The development of online distribution has activated a long-tail economy and overheated competition has made it difficult to notice differences between products. Moreover, consumer needs have grown extremely individualized, and the standardized mass-market approach is no longer helpful for businesses to have an competitive edge in the market. What businesses need now is a specialization strategy that can make each customer feel that they are buying a product or service that is "made just for me." The word "specialization" is often interchangeably used to mean "differentiation." However, "differentiation" is a business management strategy that deals with the strengths of a company or its rival company, whereas specialization is more like a business management tactic that is more detailed and consumer-oriented.

Specialization begins not with competitors or skills, but from understanding customers. Differentiation alone is not enough. Businesses must come up with products, services, and markets that are sure to be a perfect fit for customers, like the glass slipper that fit only Cinderella's foot. To make this happen, businesses have to carefully observe the target customers, segment them into groups to narrow down the targeted range, and come up with specialization strategies to satisfy each group. A reasonable and precise segmentation strategy is important for specialization, and this strategy requires four figurative tools: tweezers, a microscope, a compass, and a fishing rod.

You need tweezers to identify and pick out a market where you want to specialize by observing "customer characteristics"; a microscope to identify "customer needs" that are randomly distributed; a compass to focus on the characteristics of the "region" by drawing concentric circles on the map; and a fishing rod to provide a lure for customers who want to focus on your "one" capability.

1. The Tweezers Strategy: Specializing for Customer Characteristics

Lefty's, a brand that started as a small neighborhood store and has grown to the point where it has a store in Disney World, is a retailer that sells products made only for left-handed consumers, as indicated by its name. Left-handed consumer account for only about 10~15 percent of the total population. Targeting a small set of consumers is a different model from most businesses, which generally start out by targeting the biggest consumer base possible. Lefty's is an example of a business that succeeded by accurately targeting and penetrating a niche market that clearly exists, albeit on a small scale. Another good example is Vegemil Soymilk for 5060 Seniors, a product specialized for people in their 50s and 60s. It was launched in 2017 and recorded 10 million units in sales in just two years. The number of packages sold is equivalent to 73 percent of the 13.6 million aged between 50-69 in Korea.[2] The company succeeded in specialization by adding "5060 Seniors" in the name of the product to indicate it was a healthy beverage with additional nutritional ingredients for the health and vitality of middle to old aged consumers. The success of this soymilk product was possible because the company carefully considered the age of the consumers, their nutritional needs, and the flavors they like the most.

While travel has become a national leisure pastime, related industries are also striving to launch target-specific products. Businesses are striving to segment consumer bases in further detail to keep pace with rapidly changing travel trends, which include the MZ generation (collective name of the Millennial and Z generations) consumers who prefer "staying vacation" over "getting away vacation" and travelers who prefer Airbnb, which promises maximum local experience over hotels.

For example, Shilla Hotel신라호텔in Jeju has introduced a package exclusively for single travelers. This package is sold in summer, which is a peak traveling season. This shows how a target-specific specialized product has become a success in the mainstream market, instead of just in a niche market.

2. The Microscope Strategy: Specializing for Customer Needs

Since the 1990s, many groups of people who came to be known as "a tribe" have been born, such as the yuppies and the nomads. Now, it has become very common for a certain group of people to be named in similar fashion based on their shared values, lifestyles, and tastes, such as the YOLOs, a group of people who believe in "you only live once"; the Coffices, a group of people who enjoy working in cafes while drinking coffee; and the Photoshooters. These groups of consumers hold a key to specialization. The microscope strategy begins with meticulous market research to identify the specific needs and values that they pursue.

Office-sharing services have been growing rapidly throughout the world including Korea since the world's first office sharing service, Coworking Space launched in San Francisco, US, in 2005. The first office-sharing service in Korea, Fast Five, launched in 2015, and it was soon followed by numerous other similar office-sharing services. Recently, shared workspace for people working in the same industry had grown popular. In the U.S. and Europe, there are booming workspace sharing businesses that target segmented groups of people who share similar occupations and interests, a few examples of which include: Tradecraft Industries that is specialized in architect consumers; Orega in media industry; Law Firm Suites which is work space in legal businesses ; and Karma Kitchen in the food and beverage industry. In Korea, there is Musinsa Studio무신사 스튜디오 which is found in the Dongdaemun area known to be the center of fashion in Korea and mostly occupied by fashion-related businesses; Finß핀베타 which is run by Hyundai Card mostly for startups in the financial industry; and WeCook, which is specialized for startups in the food and beverage industry. It seems to be inevitable for all the many workspace-sharing businesses to carry out specialization strategies to concentrate focus on their targets.

In the wake of growing awareness by consumers about issues of fairness, fairness-related consumer needs have been emerging in various industries. One example is fair travel. Travelus Map, a travel agency under the banner of fair travel, offers sustainable fair travel products that do not damage the environment of the travel destinations. In order to reduce the adverse effects of over-tourism, such as environmental destruction and inflation, the company organizes trips for smaller group, and tourists walk or use public transportation. One of the goals of the fair travel packages offered by this company is creation of income for the locals by proactively utilizing local businesses, such as restaurants, lodgings, and experience programs run by local residents. The packages are also limited to fewer than 15 travelers per group to prevent damage to tourist sites, and these travelers use eco-friendly transportation such as public transportation, bicycles and walking. While this kind of tour may be a bit inconvenient compared to conventional travel packages, these fair travel packages are well received by conscious consumers who support the objectives of fair travel. Those who have experienced these travel packages are becoming return customers.

3. The Compass Strategy: Specializing by Commercial District

In conventional offline business, commercial districts were usually analyzed in terms of location factors such as demographics, traffic, and transportation, as well as the status and characteristics of businesses operating in those districts, before deciding the size of the commercial districts. But this traditional analysis of commercial districts is changing. One example is the rise of the Compass Commercial District, which covers only the area within a circle that is similar to a circle drawn with a compass needle secured on one target point. Recently, the diameter of this compass circle is growing smaller.

Specialization strategies for different commercial districts are manifested, for example, in their different business hours. All banks used to open from 9:00 a.m to 4:00 p.m throughout every region in Korea but now, they are introducing flexible business hours to fit regional characteristics. The change in business hours also becomes a means to overcome crises faced by conventional banks in the wake of growing untact business transactions through popular mobile banking and Internet-only online banks. KEB Hana Bank opened a specialized branch in Gwangsan, Gwangju, for alien workers and inter-cultural families who reside in the neighborhood. The bank opens even on Sundays for those alien workers and foreign-born residents who have difficulties in visiting banks during workdays. Shinhan Bank is also running branches specialized in serving foreigners in five regions across the country, including Seoul's Daerim-dong and Uijeongbu, and has staffed those branches with employees who are fluent in Vietnamese, Thai and Russian to communicate with them smoothly. KB Kookmin Bank has been increasing its branches specialized in commercial districts and now stay open until 5:00 p.m., 6:00 p.m. and 7:00 p.m. respectively for workers or business customers who have difficulty visiting banks during working hours.

For franchises or distributors who have many outlets across the country, specialization by commercial district has a particular significance. In the past, standardization was a virtue because it allowed companies to provide the same quality of products and services at affordable prices throughout the country, but now adaptability is more important because it allows companies to be flexible in providing products and services that are best suited to each of the different commercial districts they operate in.

Businesses are making efforts to transform uniform branches to specialized ones according to local characteristics.

For example, Lotte Mart started offering different products in different outlet types depending on the main customers of the respective business zones instead of opening more outlets. The decision reflected their declining sales as a result of growing food delivery businesses. In the Seocho district, Seoul, which is a high-income area with a higher population in their 20s than the national average, the company designed the outlet for customers who enjoy grocery shopping and cooking themselves. In the Songpa and Gangnam districts with higher population in their 30s and 40s with children and relatively higher income, the company opened outlets that specialize in eco-friendly organic produce.

When the family restaurant business started losing ground in the wake of a growing number of people who are dining alone, CJ Food Ville overhauled the company's restaurant brand VIPS and opened restaurants specialized for business zones in an effort to change the direction of the business. VIPS in office areas specialize in salads, while the central branch in Myeong-dong marked by heavy traffic of career men and women and college students in their 20~30s has a microbrew specializing corner where customers can drink the beer as much as they want. In fact, after the branch reopened as a specialized restaurant, it recorded a six fold increase in sales.[3]

We are not simply in an era of customer satisfaction; we are in an era of customer hyper-satisfaction. The niche becomes the rich. Narrow down, cut down, and sharpen your edge.

4. The Fishing Rod Strategy: Specializing for Corporate Competitiveness

No perm, no hair dying, and not even a hair cutting service. Only the hair drying service is available. This is what is happening at a chain hair salon specializing only in drying hair, Drybar, which already has over 100 hair salons in the US. Committed to offering "only one service but in the best way," Drybar is the leader in the shampoo and blow-dry business. Their main target is career women in big cities. Even though Drybar offers only a simple shampooing and blow-drying service, it is so popular that making a reservation is a challenge,

Gentle Monster젠틀몬스터, an eyeglass brand that has attracted the attention of people from all over the world with its gallery-like showrooms, has demonstrated exceptional talent in unraveling experimental and unconventional space design in its showrooms. The Korean brand launched with just five employees in 2011, but now it has grown into a global brand with six overseas affiliates, and investment from luxury group LVMH. The brand's biggest success factor was the specialized showroom. The brand's showrooms play the role of serving as windows that deliver the company's values, message and sensibility beyond being the channel that sells goods. Their commitment in specialized space design is evident in the fact that 80 out of 150 employees at the headquarters are dedicated to space design. Such obsession with space design has been the most important factor for Gentle Monster to grow into a global brand.

The food delivery service, Baedal Minjok배달의민족 (a/k/a Baemin, lit. The People of Delivery), is another good example with cutting-edge specialization strategy. Baemin seized the market as a brand specializing in humor while spreading the brand's identity and values through humorous codes. For this brand, being humorous is a kind of specialization tactic. The company revealed a witty sense of humor and fun designs through collaborating events with other brands, such as Baemin Spring Literature Contest; Baemin Stationeries collaborated with the retail company 10x10; Baemin Fashion collaborated with fashion designers; and Your Order of Cup Coffee collaborated with 7-Eleven. Baemin's humor codes that seem freewheeling yet stay within the line, and Baemin's designs that match those humor codes were the biggest contributors to making the company the leader in the industry both in terms of brand awareness and sales.

Implications

There was a time when standardization was a virtue, because providing the same products and services that ensure the same quality anywhere was something only large corporations, conglomerates or chains with a lot of capital and elaborate systems could do. But now, in addition to standardized tastes, there exist a wide variety of "individual tastes" that need to be satisfied. Assured satisfaction of a select few has become more important than appealing to all customers.

This environmental cause can be seen as the background behind the recent rise in interest in agile methodologies that allow companies to respond to these changes with more flexibility. The fast ones, not the strong ones, will survive. It is the time when fast followers who used to follow previous success models need to come up with a new winning strategy. Instead of following what everyone else does, they need to respond with alertness and agility in a business environment, in which nobody can predict what will change and when, if they want to survive.

Instead of following others, businesses need to identify an area to be specialized, split it up as much as they can, and find their own competitive edge in the process. They should be able to look at the market deeply and narrowly to pull out an essential value that has the capacity for successful specialization. This requires them to become "agile movers." Agile movers continuously self-generate the engine for specialization while pursuing satisfactionism, instead of perfectionism, all based on constant practice and experience.

"Customer satisfaction" is now a cliché. Instead of trying to appeal to random, unspecified people who may or may not have interests in your company and products, it is more effective to focus exclusively on those few who show clear interest. For this reason, it is also important to have an assessment tool to measure the satisfaction of those targeted customers. More attention and research are needed in how customer satisfaction leads to a rise in sales and profit.

The niche becomes the rich. Narrow down, cut down, and sharpen your edge. Only the specialized will survive.

Iridescent OPAL

the New 5060 Generation

A new generation is emerging in the consumer market. The group of consumers born in the 1950s and 1960s, which includes baby boomers, was until recently considered old and insignificant in the consumer market, but this group is now emerging as the "new middle-aged group." These people believe they are in the heyday of their lives, and consequently they can be called "Generation OPAL." OPAL stands for "Old People with Active Lives." More than anything, the term embraces the idea that the colorful characteristics these people display resemble the opal gemstone, which is said to contain the colors of all gemstones. This new middle-aged group of consumers in their 50s and 60s — the baby boomers — are named "Generation OPAL."

Generation OPAL has left their old jobs but is taking up the challenge of working in new jobs. They also enjoy dynamic leisure activities, knowing that every moment counts ever more as they get older. Furthermore, they form new consumer trends while following the tastes and brands of younger generations, and they purchase their own content products, consequently bringing the winds of change to various industries. The OPAL generation is actually a very diverse and picky consumer group. Simply offering larger fonts and easy-to-use features cannot appeal to the OPAL generation. Companies need to approach the generation with detailed consideration of segmented lifestyles. Who calls them stubborn old folks? No more stereotype image of elders. The OPAL generation, who vigorously uses YouTube and new technologies as freely as younger people, is playing a key role in society and will provide fresh energy to the stagnant market.

- Debuted as the first senior model in Korea at the F/W Hera Seoul Fashion Week KIMMY.J show in 2018.
- Appeared in various entertainment and cultural TV programs, fashion shows, and magazine covers
- Modeled for various food and retail brands not to mention men's wear, outdoor wear, SPA and other clothing brands.
- Boasts 72,000 Instagram followers as of October 2019.
- The future goal is to walk the runway in the world's top four fashion week events.

Kim Chil-doo, one of the most popular models in Korea, has a very impressive career record. At 65, he is in the heyday of his life. If compared to a gemstone, he is more like an opal that boasts beautiful and diverse colors as rich as the clothes he wears on stage, rather than silver, the color of his mustache. The Korean baby boomers, himself included, are already in their late 50s and mid-60s. They were the main players behind the rapid economic growth of Korea, and they are still socially and economically active. They are living their second heyday. They enjoy challenging hobbies, and they are not willing to fall behind the latest trends. Silver and gray, the traditional colors of the older generation do not apply to those in their 50s and 60s any more. The colorful characteristics these people display resembles rather the colorful opal gemstone, and a more apropos name for them is "Generation Opal."

With regard to Generation OPAL, the word "opal" has many meanings. First, OPAL could stand for "Old People with Active Lives," a term first introduced in Japan in 2002 to refer to active seniors who are emerging as the pillar in an aging society.[1] In Korean, the word "opal" is also pronounced the same as the number "58," so the term can also conveniently refer to those who were born in "1958, the Year of the Dog," representing the baby boomers. Moreover, the opal gemstone is often considered the most perfect precious gemstone because it allegedly shows different colors depending on the angle because it contains the colors of all gemstones including sapphire blue, emerald green, topaz yellow, ruby red and amethyst purple. In this book, the new middle-aged group of consumers in their 50s and 60s − the Korean baby boomers − are named "Generation OPAL" to embrace the idea that the colorful characteristics these people display resemble the colorful opal gemstone. Simply put, Generation OPAL is the new title for the group of people in their 50s and 60s who are finally displaying their colors in the new millennium.

The OPAL generation is retired people, and after finishing their first act of life as a parent with the independence of their children, they are now actively and progressively opening the second act of life without being burdened by the many roles that they'd played both at home and society for most of their lives.

Finally being able to enjoy life for themselves, they look for the joy of passion instead of the duty of labor, care more about happiness today than tomorrow, and invest lavishly for their health, beauty and quality of life. They are not much different from young people when it comes to shopping online and communicating with the world through YouTube.

A New Name: The OPAL Generation

In Korea, "baby boomers" refer to those born between 1955 and 1963, whose are the result of a sharp increase in birth rates following the end of the Korean War. Their birth rates topped out at more than 800,000 per year, and now, their total population is more than 7.11 million (as of the 2015 census). The higher birth rate continued for a while after the births of the baby boomers, and if we consider a slightly wider range and count those currently in their 50s and 60s, they form a huge group that makes up 28 percent of the Korean population. But their strong presence in society is not simply due to their large number. When they were younger, the country developed rapidly, with a high level of economic growth at around 10%. They currently hold the biggest assets among all age groups, and they are still the mainstay of Korean society because they are supporting their adult children (one out of every two households) and their aging parents (six out of every ten households).

What kind of consumers are baby boomers? They have a strong belief in good education because they observed a strong correlation between level of education and income level in post-war Korean society. Having been the main players behind the rapid industrialization of Korea, they are also achievement-oriented people. Frugality is an integral part of their character because they remember the times when supplies were scarce after the Korean War. Upholding traditional values, they believe that supporting family is their duty. These are their well-known traits. However, their current lifestyles are quite multi-faceted and it is difficult to grasp the whole picture from this existing knowledge alone. They are born as baby boomers due to the timing of their birth, but they are now becoming generation OPAL due to the joint contribution of their unique life style and the increasing prevalence of IT technology.

The New Middle-Aged and Older Generation: a New Definition of Seniors

Until now, adulthood has been divided into three age groups: youth, middle age and old age. Our accepted view of the life cycle was that in your middle-age years, you raised your children and supported your parents, and when you enter your 60s, you retire and leave your job. The old age years were believed to be a time you lived the later years of your life while being supported by your children or with the money you'd saved for life after retirement.

But Korean society is now redefining this new period of later years of life. With life expectancy extending at a pace unprecedented in the world, Koreans have more post-retirement years than before to continue their social activities in good health. Furthermore, as the younger generations are getting married or finding jobs much later than before, the old age group find themselves having to support their children longer than before. And the extending life expectancy means they also have to support their aging parents longer as well. This series of changes is forcing many Koreans who belong to the old age population to enter the job market again.

"The new middle-aged group of people신중년층" is a new term used by the younger generations to refer to these groups of adults whose characteristics don't exactly match the conventional sense of the middle-aged and senior populations. As they enter a new stage of life that is different from the past, they start showing a way of life that is similar to that of the younger generation. Unlike their counterparts of the past, these new groups of aged people have already departed from their social and occupational roles that used to define them and set off on a self-discovery journey with higher will and interests in their hobbies and tastes. When choosing a job, fun and self-realization matters to them more than before as well.

Mobile Makes Them Grab the World in Their Hands

Even though baby boomers have been adapting to the turbulent history of Korean society, IT technology, which has developed rapidly over the last decade, has in many ways caused differences in the way of life between generations. However, as the mobile ecosystem matures and is allowing users to do a lot more with much simpler manipulation than PCs, the baby boomers, once called the analog generation, naturally became capable of jumping on the bandwagon of the mobile generation through platforms such as Kakao Talk and YouTube.

According to the 2017 Internet Usage Survey conducted by the Korea Internet Development Institute, the rate of mobile Internet use reached 97.6 percent among the users in their 50s and 81.2 percent among the users in their 60s. The change is also confirmed by the actual amount of data used by consumers. In the first quarter of 2019, consumers aged 50 and older turned out to have used 3.1GB of data per month. This is more than a two-fold increase from the 1.5GB data used as of the first quarter of 2016. Their increase rate was faster than their counterparts between the ages of 10~40.[2] The background of these changes can be found in the expanding influence of YouTube. According to the app analytics firm, WiseApp, 26 percent of the 38.8 billion minutes Koreans spent on YouTube were accounted for by those in their 50s or older as of April 2019.[3] That means the time users in their 50s and older spend on YouTube has doubled compared to the same period a year earlier. Now the OPAL generation is communicating with the world more easily through YouTube, and it is only natural that they are undergoing quantitative and qualitative changes in the entire process of consumption, from searching for product information to purchasing a product.

A Myriad of Colors of the OPAL Generation

1. Finding the Hidden Place: Accepting the Challenge to Find New Jobs

For the OPAL generation who are leaving their long-held jobs, retirement does not mean leaving the stage altogether. To them, retirement does not mean leaving behind all social activities and moving on to a leisurely life in seclusion. Work is the most important keyword that distinguishes the OPAL generation from previous older generations. The OPAL generation is a group of new middle-aged people who are proactively exploring yet another area through new work, not a group of the elderly who are living a passive lifestyle.

The 2017 data from the National Statistical Office showed that more than seven out of 10 people (71.7%) between the age of 50 and 69 want to continue working after retiring from their main jobs. Their desire to keep working and engaging in social activities during this new phase of their life cycle is closely related to their consumption patterns. In today's consumer society, consumption is essential to maintain self-identity and a desirable lifestyle. Therefore, consumption becomes an important motivation for people to work and generate income after retirement.

Continuing social activities as well as these economic needs makes a big difference in their bio rhythms and life itself. Therefore, the OPAL generation's demands for products and services are also different from those of senior citizens of the past. In particular, if they are working in an office environment, they are very likely to have been exposed to new IT technologies while performing their jobs, regardless of their ages. That is the reason they easily play along with trends instead of being alienated from changes happening in the new social environment.

Therefore, for the OPAL generation who begin the second chapter of life, work is no longer the only means of sustenance. Those who had quietly performed their roles and duties in pre-retirement life began to unfold the dreams they never had a chance to unfold before. Kim Childoo, the senior model introduced previously, started his modeling career in his 60s after running a small restaurant for 27 years. Another YouTuber, Simbanggol Housewife심방골주부, was also just an ordinary housewife in her late 50s who enjoyed cooking, but she is reborn as a famous YouTube creator after she started posting videos of her cooking homemade dishes. The creator of the YouTube channel with over 40,000 subscribers, Mr. Chasan's Common Legal Knowledge차산선생 법률상식, is a retired former Supreme Court justice.

With the development of the platform economy, the OPAL generation has more opportunities than ever to use their skills and talents. The popularity is growing in experience-sharing platforms that link the experiences and know-how of seniors to the industries or people who need them. Furthermore, there is a dynamic trend of recycling professional human resources as well. For example, Talent Bank탤런트 뱅크 connects former corporate executive-level and higher professionals with extensive experience and backgrounds in ten areas – business management strategies, new business lines, sales & purchasing, HR, labor issues, marketing and IT – with small and medium sized companies. In just a year after its official launching of the service, the company recorded 500 successful matching projects, and a 60 percent return customer rate, thereby proving the value of the OPAL generation.[4]

2. Believing in YOLO: Time is More Precious in Older Years

One of the important interests of the OPAL Generation is time management. They lived a dynamic and busy life when they were younger, and they do not waste their time in the second round of their life in retirement. Therefore, many retirees enjoy leisure activities as if they were professionals still on the job. Their week passes by quickly while they exercise to improve health, take various classes at cultural centers for self-improvement, cultivate their hobbies to realize their old dreams of becoming a writer or a painter, and take care of family members and neighbors. For the OPAL generation, spare time does not mean leisurely time with little activity. Spare time is time they can invest in themselves by experiencing the things they previously did not, or could not, experience when they were younger.

The OPAL generation is happily spending their precious time in travelling, too. They are the true YOLOs who are willing to pack and leave for famous tourist destinations around the country or around the world as much as they can. According to a survey, 84.5 percent of people over the age of 50 answered that traveling was the first thing they wanted to pursue a happy life.[5] As more seniors are willing to open their wallets for traveling, more premium tour packages are becoming available in the market to meet older people's higher expectations. One such package was a Latin America tour that CJ O Shopping, a home shopping company, sold during the Korean Thanksgiving long weekend. At almost $10,000 per head, the package was expensive, but about 730 viewers called in to buy the package during the one-hour TV program. It exceeded their sales goal by 177%. Lotte Home Shopping has introduced a Western Mediterranean Cruise package, and GS Home Shopping has introduced an Iceland Tour package, further fueling the race for premium travel packages.

Their travel destinations evolve, too. While in the past, they might have seen a TV program about a famous tourist destination and become motivated to tour that place themselves, now, they look for places that offer experiences that they've never had before, and travel as far and long as they can handle. Travel methods are also evolving as more and more consumers in their 50s and 60s have accumulated travel experience. Like an insurance planner who designs complex insurance products to suit individual needs, the travel agents are becoming more like "experience designers" who add a little extra, such as a short in-between tour or local tour to the existing travel packages to suit those tour consumers' tastes.

Traveling without a guide is not uncommon either. Having become adept at using smart phones, the OPAL generation tourists often set off on a tour of Europe as a couple by renting a car and relying on Google map and translator apps.

The OPAL generation being a group of active seniors who are eager to live to the fullest in doing both daily and non-daily activities, they are also dynamically involved in cultural activities. In fact, a survey of Seoul citizens showed that the ratio of people who have watched any cultural or art performance more than once a year was 77 percent for men and 89 percent for women in their 50s and 60s, the highest among all age groups. The average number of performances that they watched in a year was 6.7, which was similar to those in their 20s, according to the survey. On top of this, the improved ability to use mobile devices is also changing the daily landscape of the OPAL generation. They are just as good as younger generations in online searching of famous restaurants, exhibitions, and various discount information across the country. It is not uncommon to see women from the OPAL generation visiting hot places to enjoy the atmosphere during workday hours after the customers in their 20s and 30s are gone.

3. "Passed Up" Consumer Behavior: OPAL Becoming the Mainstay of the Market

People think that as you grow older, you don't like changes, and you rarely take up any new adventures in terms of consumption because your patterns of life have already been formed. But this long-held stereotype is unraveling. The OPAL generation may change slower than the younger generations, but they are willing to use their time and effort to catch up with changes as long as the changes are deemed worthwhile. Online shopping businesses are dynamically reacting to the growing number of the so-called "silver surfers" and "the webbers" who have grown accustomed to the convenience of mobile shopping. According to Auction, an online shopping service in Korea, the sales volumes of all items from 2014 to the first half of 2018 by age group, the consumers in their 50s showed a 130 percent increase, and in their 60s, 171 percent, the highest increases among all age groups.

In terms of the proportion of customers, those in their 50s and 60s also recorded a sharp increase from 17 percent in 2014 to 27 percent in 2018. When analyzed by item, their purchase of travel and flight tickets made an 11-fold increase (1,040 percent), high-end brand clothing, seven-fold increase (683 percent), and luxury brand imports, two-fold increase (184 percent), thereby proving that their major purchases are expanding from daily necessities to luxury brand items.[6]

With the growing number of "silver surfers" who try to solve all shopping needs through mobile devices, the related industries are dynamically responding to the needs of senior consumers. Hyundai Department Store has overhauled the company's mobile platform by increasing the font size of the mobile app by up to 30 percent and more than doubling the number of images, while the simple payment system Kakao Pay has also enhanced visual accessibility by modifying the contrast and alternative text on the app and showcasing easy-to-understand service design and intuitive images. As a result, the number of users over the age of 60 has more than doubled compared to the previous year.[7]

Now, consumption behaviors are passed up, instead of down, between generations. The changes in consumption of the OPAL Generation are also evident in data. Among the CJ ONE members who visit the drugstore Olive Young 올리브영, whose major target is consumers in their 20s and 30s, the proportion of sales to consumers aged 40 and older is continuously increasing. The portion of sales to those middle-aged consumers was 6.8 percent for the entire year of 2012, but it reached double digits with 10.9 percent in 2014, and it recorded 20.7 percent in the first half of 2018. Their main purchasing items were health supplements such as vitamins and minerals, but now, they are buying color makeup such as nail stickers and lip tints, which are popular among millennials.[8]

Likewise, there is an increasing number of OPAL generation consumers who are paying attention to the *convenium* services

Who calls them stubborn old folks?
Get rid of that stereotype. The OPAL generation,
who uses the internet and new technologies as
freely as younger people, is playing a key role
in society and will provide fresh energy to the
stagnant market.

that are popular among the younger generations as well. The number of people who are in their 50s and subscribing to the food delivery service Market Kurly마켓컬리 made almost a 10 fold increase as of the first half of 2018 compared to the previous year. That means, consumers in their 50s and over who have increased access to mobile shopping have begun to actively join the consumers who are using services verified by younger generations.

4. What's Wrong with Trot?: The Changing Landscape of the Content Market

The content market is also moving and shaking depending on the response of the OPAL generation. In the movie market, the movie Bohemian Rhapsody recorded 9.94 million cumulative ticket sales in the second half of 2018 and became a box office hit after word of mouth provoked nostalgia among the middle-aged and older audiences. In the music market, the timeless steady-seller music genre among the middle-aged and older music fans, the trot (a genre of Korea's traditional pop song), is making a glorious revival. The TV program, *Tomorrow's Miss Trot*, which targeted the music tastes of those older generations recorded the highest viewer rating among entertainment programs with an average viewer rating of 18.1 percent. The nationwide concert tour which featured all the contestants also swept from first to fifth places on a major ticket reservation ranking.

As mentioned previously, the impact of the integrated video sharing platforms through YouTube is also significant. With so many middle-aged people turning to YouTube for listening to music, trot genre music content can easily record millions of views and a trot singer who became popular on YouTube was crowned as the "President of middle-aged people." After a large number of online users in their 50s and 60s started visiting YouTube, they make their presence felt by having their favorite videos on current affairs and politics ranking up in the list of videos that became popular within a short time. The OPAL generation is good at finding YouTube videos on issues they are interested in.

Implications

Older consumers were often called "the New Silver Generation" and "the Active Seniors" but that is also constantly changing. The English word "senior" means older, or in higher level, but now middle-aged and older consumers refuse to be defined as "senior," because they consider themselves not much different from their younger counterparts. They identify themselves with those in their 30s or 40s, even though they are a little older than them. In fact, the lifestyles of the OPAL generation are not much different from those of the younger generations. Even after retirement, many of them keep interacting with those who belong to their children's generation and remain in the cities, all of which make their lifestyles not much different from those of the millennials and become susceptible to changes. While there are still differences in values such as family relationships and being frugal, we need to drop the bias about people in their 50s and 60s as being an outsider group.

As a consumer group, the OPAL generation is actually a very complex and picky crowd. Just because the OPAL consumers are familiar with mobile technology and the millennials' lifestyles, this does not mean they want exactly the same products and services that millennials want. Difficulties and inconveniences in getting used to new things are still a large barrier to embracing change. Kakao Talk and YouTube were able to reach out to the OPAL generation successfully because these services are really not that difficult to use. Completely new products and services are not appealing to them. Instead, businesses should aim to offer considerate and tailored products and services that can allow the OPAL generation to keep doing what they did when they were younger.

Professor Joseph F. Coughlin, founder of MIT AgeLab, used Harley-Davidson as an example to describe this strategy. When the average age of their customers reached 50, the U.S.

motorcycle maker Harley-Davidson lowered the saddle height and built in a control board that was easy to manually operate so that those with a smaller build – women and seniors – can have a pleasant riding experience.[9] Instead of a massive marketing campaign for senior customers, the company employed a subtle strategy to appeal to senior customers. In the same sense, businesses need to break away from the idea that a separate business line is necessary for older customers. Generation OPAL does not want something entirely new. They just want products and services that improve everyday happiness and convenience.

Convenium

Convenience as a Premium

Convenience is premium. As the standard of purchase is shifting from cost-effectiveness to premiums, the elements of being premium are changing. The new standard for premiums for modern consumers — who have many things they want to do but not enough time to do them all — is anything that provides maximum performance with minimum effort and time. There are three "convenium" strategies: (1) Help customers cut down the absolute time required to carry out a task; (2) Help customers save effort required to carry out a task; and (3) Help customers maximize the outcome they want.

It is a characteristic of the times that convenience has become a crucial element of being premium. Today's young consumers are always short of time. Nevertheless, they want to invest their precious time in new experiences and self-growth. Moreover, in today's society of weak personal ties, where people find it difficult to ask neighbors or relatives for small favors, people are forced to solve their problems on their own, whether big or small. For these reasons, consumers are willing to open their wallet if some products or services can save them time and effort. Another factor is that shortage of available jobs has increased the number of young job seekers and retirees who are willing to work as "bridge workers." These people are flowing into the platform labor market without much restriction.

The convenium market is expected to grow at a fast pace. Improving trust among consumers, workers and platforms is the first order of business. Focus on the minor inconveniences of consumers and make their lives a premium. People say we are in a bad recession, but opportunities still exist.

Today's customers are always short on time, and thus they highly value efficiency in their daily lives. Living in an atomized society with looser personal ties, people today are also forced to solve their problems on their own, whether big or small. Moreover, the app economy built on smartphone applications is expanding rapidly. When considering all these together, we can expect that the 2020 version of "being premium" will be all about ensuring convenience for customers. In other words, if businesses can understand and implement exactly what it takes to deliver convenience to their customers through their products or services, businesses can successfully use "premium strategies" and convince consumers to pay a higher price. Because the trend of convenience is the core factor of premium products and services, this trend can be named "convenium."

Today's consumers are smart. They spend their time and effort on essential tasks that they must do themselves, but for all other tasks they look for someone else who can do those tasks for them. Today's consumers have no reservations about using services that save time and effort for them, or drastically improve their efficiency. They mostly use products and services that offer more convenience for them in daily chores and activities, such as housekeeping, cleaning, or standing in line to buy something. The "convenium" market is naturally growing as single-person households and working couples who are always running short of time are becoming the main consumer bases. In their busy daily lives, people today are willing to pay more in exchange for saved time and convenience. The following are successful premium services and strategies that are chosen by "smart but lazy" consumers.

Strategies for a Better Convenium

Convenience became a premium factor because saving the "time and effort" required to do little annoying chores became more important than ever. Now, sharpening a competitive edge is all about helping customers save time by paying a little extra money and using the time they save to have other diverse experiences. When experience matters more than possession, "extra time" that allows you to travel abroad is more valuable than owning a luxury bag. Being able to buy some extra time and convenience is no longer the result of laziness on the consumers' side; it is the choice consumers make for a premium lifestyle. When it comes to convenium, you can improve the efficiency of convenience by increasing the outcome itself or by cutting down the required time and effort needed. If made into a formula, it is as follows.

Convenium = Achievements / (Efforts x Time)

Therefore, in order to enhance convenience, we need to reduce the effort or time denominator, or increase the outcome numerator. So the question is: What are the necessary strategies to make it happen?

1. The Time-saving Fast Track Strategy

The first strategy of convenium is to save customers time to increase convenience. One good example of this strategy can be found on YouTube: the "skip" option to skip pre-roll advertisements after five seconds. However, there are still ads that cannot be skipped or sometimes multiple ads are shown in a row. People who want to save even those few seconds of time choose YouTube Premium service, a paid service that allows people to watch videos without having to watch ads at the cost of 7,900 won per month. YouTube Premium has other features such as downloading videos, but the key to this service is the removal of ads. For those who do not want to waste even just a few seconds required to watch ads before pressing the 'skip' button, it is a more reasonable option to pay extra money to save time.

Parents with infants and toddlers all know that having an extra helping hand, or the right equipment, can make a huge difference. The key selling point of baby care products is how much free time they can offer to parents. Some of these items include a hands-free breast pump that allows mothers to do other things while collecting breast milk; an automatic milk formula maker that saves the time required to mix baby formula; and a bottle sterilizer that reduces the time to sterilize baby bottles. Those are the items that opened a new premium business line with the promise of "saving time" in the parenting market where hygiene and safety have been the top selling point.

These are examples that show how consumers are increasingly responding positively to something that helps them save time drastically. A good example in the food and beverage market is the "smart order" through which customers can order food or drinks using smartphones or other mobile devices. In the case of Starbucks, the Siren Order service allows customers to order without having to stand in long lines or go to the counter. This reduced waiting time not only increases customer satisfaction but also turnover at the store.

Starbucks was followed by most other coffee chains, such as A Twosome Place, Ediya Coffee, Tom N Toms, and Hollys Coffee. They all have implemented their own version of a smart order system. Starbucks received 66 million smart orders in 2018, filling 18 percent of all daily orders. Now that the company's smart order system has proven its effectiveness, similar services are quickly spreading to other businesses in the industry such as Lotteria and KFC.[1]

Reducing the required time to complete a task is one way to save time, but there is another way to save time: multitasking. One good example of this strategy is audio book services, which help customers read a book not with their eyes but with their ears. According to GoodEReader. com, the global audio book market recorded a 20.5 percent annual increase from $2 billion in 2013 to $3.5 billion in 2016. These figures are notable when compared with the 1.9 percent growth in the print book market during the same period. This so-called "multitasking reading" allows readers to do other things while listening to a book as if they are listening to a radio, without having to hold the book with their hands. In fact, according to a survey conducted by the U.S. Audio Publishers Association in June 2017, consumers listed the ability to multitask as an important reason for using audio book services.

The audio book market is also slowly heating up in Korea as well. Millie's Study밀리의서재, Korea's most popular reading app available for a monthly fixed subscription fee, reported that when Yuval Noah Harari's *Sapiens: A Brief History of Humankind* was made into an audio book with the voice of actor Lee Byung-hun, 1,500 subscribers listened to the audio book in just one week after it was made available. According to Audien Sound오디언소리, Korea's largest audio book production and distribution company, the number of paid subscribers of audio books reached 351,428 as of the second quarter of 2019, up 377 percent from 74,552 a year earlier.[2]

2. The Effort-saving Streamlining Strategy

The second strategy for convenium is to save effort. It is a strategy for consumers who are more intent on applying themselves to do things that they can do better than others and hire somebody to do other chores. In particular, consumers are willing to pay money to have experts do housekeeping chores for them. The services are as diverse as the customer demands in this industry.

The most noticeable in this industry is the errand service. Kim Jipsa김집사 (lit. Butler Kim) is an errand service platform claiming to take care of "all errands within 20 minutes, starting at 2,000 won." This service can have somebody do all the annoying housekeeping chores such as throwing away garbage, delivering food and groceries, picking up laundry, and going to the post office for mail. The errand apps, which started with simple cleaning or grocery shopping services, have recently expanded the range of services offered to standing in line to purchase tickets for famous concerts

Consumers are more intent on applying themselves to do things that they can do better than others and hire somebody to do other chores like errands and house cleaning.

and even creating PowerPoint presentations. You can even order a service to take care of an inmate for you.

Daerijubu대리주부 (literally, surrogate housewife), Miso미소, and Home Master홈마스터 are among other home cleaning services that have recently appeared. Home Master has photos and work experience of their trained housekeeping experts available for viewing, so that customers can pick one that they like. Daerijubu, the No. 1 housekeeping service provider in this industry, has recorded 53 billion won of cumulative sales as of 2018. The company's main customers are those who want to save their energy on housekeeping and use that saved energy in more productive activities for them, like playing with their children.

There are also parenting services that specialize in surrogately filling the role of mothers for working moms, whose work schedule makes it hard for them to be there for their children when they need them. The service is affordable because customers request hour-by-hour services only when they need them. Customers can also have peace of mind when using the service because these services do a meticulous background check on their personnel and train them professionally as well. One of the service providers, Momsitter맘시터, has 140,000 sitter members and 70,000 parent members nationwide. It costs only about 8,500 won per hour, and parents feel more comfortable about using the service because they can always check the profile of the sitter, customer reviews and background check information. As a result, Momsitter recorded 200,000 cumulative members in just two and a half years after its launching, and it is estimated that, as of April 2019, the monthly amount of transactions is over two billion won.[3]

New concept services that help customers to save time and effort when buying an apartment are also becoming premium selling points. One typical example is the apartment breakfast service. Trimage트리마제, one of the most luxurious apartment buildings located in Seongsu-dong, Seoul, is believed to be the first to offer a breakfast serving service to community facilities. In 2017, the company selected catering companies to serve breakfast and lunch, but recently, the service has been expanded to "all-day" meal service by including dinner as well. In addition to breakfast services, there are also services that offer convenience facilities such as a business lounge, book cafe, and sauna, not to mention luxury car sharing and housekeeping service. In the case of Lotte Castle Lausanne롯데캐슬 로잔, customers can book a car washing service once a week, in addition to hotel-style room maid services such as sterilizing and dry cleaning bed linens, couch and sofa once a month.[4]

There are also platforms that find pet-sitters for customers. With these services, customers can hire a dog sitter at around 20,000 won per hour. There is also a growing number of apps to have your car washed at the same time and location for your convenience as well.

3. The Performance-maximizing Efficiency Strategy

The third strategy for convenience is to have "maximum effect" with minimal effort. The health and beauty industries, in particular, are turning into a battlefield in the convenium market where customers expect the maximum results at minimal cost.

The latest high-tech therapy services that are drawing the most attention include a cooling sauna called cryotherapy, which promises burning calories and dramatic recovery of body condition by having the body go through a self-recovery process in extremely cold temperatures ranging between minus 110~130℃. EMS (Electronic Muscle Stimulation) training, which promises the desired result by exercising for 5 to 20 minutes only, is also drawing attention. EMS promises great improvement of motor efficiency in a short period of time by giving direct electromagnetic stimulation to the muscles through low frequency stimulation. It is known to have 3~4 times more calorie burning results than running or weightlifting by working out only 15 minutes according to the program, while wearing the special EMS suit. In Korea, X-PAD EMS Training, which was recently funded through the crowdfunding platform, Wadiz와디즈, is famous. It achieved 100 percent of the funding goal in just an hour and drew attention from people who are too lazy to work out.[5]

For today's women who are constantly racing against time, it is often a pain in the neck to find the time to put makeup on. It takes a lot of time to put on all different kinds of skincare products on top of the colored base makeup, and it also takes time and effort to remove them as well. As a result, efficiency and convenience that promises maximum result with shortest time is emerging as a hot issue in the beauty industry.

In fact, the drug store Olive Young올리브영 released an analysis report on their sales for the last three years, and it turned out that the sales of essence in 2018 have grown by 150 percent compared to 2016. The impressive result is believed to have been attributed to their "skip care" service which eliminated all unnecessary steps while delivering maximum results with minimal skincare management. In this case, they presented highly-condensed, high-performing essence for customers to enjoy effective skincare results with only a small amount, and it satisfied the needs of their consumers.

Another beauty product that is growing popular by giving maximum result at minimal cost is dry shampoo. Consumers just need to shake the bottle and spray it on their hair like they would with a hair mousse to make their hair look like it's just been shampooed. Australian-made cleaning puff Face Halo lets you just add water to make it wet and rub your face with it to get the same result as having used a makeup cleanser.

In fact, there are more men than women who prefer "all-in-one type" cosmetics. Among men's skin care cosmetics, the all-in-one cream that combines toner and lotion functions are the most popular. The sales records of Olive Young, Lalavla and LOHB's stores also show that the sales volume of all-in-one cosmetics for men is definitely higher than other products. Bro & Tips, a men's skin care product launched by AmorePacific, is also an "all-in-one" type cream specializing in Korean skin types, and it is popular among male customers who are too lazy to spend time on skincare, because it contains both toner and lotion in one bottle.

Background of the Rise of Convenium

Short-on-Time Consumers Who Care About Experience

Consumers who demand convenium services are mostly young parents in their 30s and 40s, especially housewives and young singles. They are the millennial generation, and they have a strong preference for convenience due to the characteristics of their lifestyles. First, the millennials are suffering from "time poverty," because they feel they don't have enough extra time for their personal use because so much is taken up by their jobs. The age group with the highest percentage of time poverty is people in their 30s, and married people have more time poverty issues than singles. Those with a spouse are said to be twice as likely to have a time poverty issue. Among people with children, particularly minors or preschool children, parents are destined to feel they are always short of time. Due to their strong desire to replace their shortage of time with time efficiency, the so-called "Three Must-Have Appliances," namely, dish washer, clothes dryer and robot cleaner, have become necessities, not a matter of choice.

Above all, they pursue a life where they can make choices based on their standards not by the standards of others. Since "my own satisfaction" matters most to them, they tend to be willing to spend the time and money it requires for their self-growth and self-improvement. Also, it is essential for them to find their own time because they prefer experiencing over owning materials. This is why they have no choice but to treat time as a precious commodity, which gave rise to the convenium trend.

Atomized Society and Ever-loosening Personal Ties

Young consumers, who use convenium services frequently, grew up with the Internet and mobile connections. They are more familiar with online interactions than offline ones. In the past, people could easily ask their neighbors to feed their dogs while they were away. But people today rarely know their next door neighbors and have little interaction with them. Therefore, people often find themselves having to solve problems on their own. In urgent situations, they rely on errand services instead of asking their neighbors. People prefer interacting with online profiles with which they can start and end an relationship as necessary, instead of having to introduce themselves and build an unnecessary relationship with neighbors.

In fact, when looking for a job, people are now used to going to online platforms where they do not know anyone or asking around casual acquaintances instead of asking their friends and relatives. Regarding how people find jobs, American sociologist Mark Granovetter has published an interesting study. We might expect that people with "strong ties" – friends, family members and close co-workers – are the main source of available job information.[6] According to Granovetter's study, however, people with strong ties are not the main source. Most of the time, friends' friends and casual acquaintances are the ones who have information that may lead one to find a job. These are the people we have "loose ties" with. We might say that our loose ties are growing stronger with the evolution of online platforms.

Gig Workers with a Career Trajectory Different from the Past

There are two areas of supply and demand in the convenium trend. There are people want to be served, and there are people who want to serve. It turns out that the convenium service providers are offering their services for diverse reasons, and they include: women whose career was interrupted; freelancers who are using their professional skills; retirees who need a "bridge labor" job; and career men and women who need a secondary source of income.

These people have something in common: their career track is different from the conventional career track as we know it. Until now, most people find their first job in their 20s and work hard to be promoted to a manager level position in their 30s. If their performance is good, they will be promoted to a higher position in their 50s where their ability to generate income will peak. But when they reach their 60s, all this career track comes to a halt and they retire.

Convenience is premium. It is a characteristic of the times that convenience has become a crucial element of being premium. Focus on the minor inconveniences of consumers and make their lives a premium. People say we are in a bad recession, but opportunities still exist.

This is the traditional career trajectory as we know it.

However, this is changing, according to Tammy Erickson, a professor at the London School of Economics. For example, a person joins a large company in his 20s and works hard building professional skills and knowledge in a field until he reaches 30. At 30, he takes a year off from work and travels. And at the age of 31, he joins a company and works on various projects, repeating the process of building work experience. Today's career men and women are not afraid to find a new job after taking a gap year during which time they recharge themselves, have time for self-reflection, and participate in volunteer work.

This form of work life is more flexible than the traditional career trajectory. As more people embrace flexible ideas about career, forms of employment are also quickly changing, and this change is creating a labor market of gig workers in convenium services.

Trust: The Requirement for Successful Convenium

Most convenium services are provided by platform workers who are working on short-term non-binding contracts. The advantage of platform businesses that connect unspecified multiple customers can sometimes turn out to be a critical disadvantage, mainly due to safety-related issues. Since both the purchasers and providers of the service are complete strangers to each other, issues regarding untrustworthy agents and consumers are emerging. These issues include personal information leaks, reliability of visiting services, and treatment of workers, but the most serious issue is that these services can be misused to commit serious crimes. In order to receive the service, a customer has to invite the service provider into their most private personal space, and this often becomes the cause of undesirable incidents. One example is a man with a history of sexual assault who joined an errand service app as a driver. He tried to rape a woman who had requested a service. The service providers are just as insecure as well. Consumers have minimal security measures because they can read other users' reviews before choosing a service provider. But the service providers don't have any such security measures when they accept a job with a client. They are exposed to dangers because they never know who they will be providing their service to, and should they become victimized by any crimes, they don't have any remedy to get compensation for their damages.

Airbnb users can pick the room or the host after reading other users' reviews and scores, and the hosts can also review the guests' information. Similarly, most consumers of platform services take the reviews and scores seriously. Trust is more important than anything particularly for parents who need somebody to care for their children. For this reason, a strategy seems to be necessary to build trust by making the process of using convenience services transparent. The users' evaluation system should be further strengthened and so should the screening of service providers. A mutual evaluation system that considers both the consumers and service providers is bound to be an important factor in successful convenium platform service.

Implications

Today, consumers are opening their wallets to buy something that helps them lead their lives in a premium way while spending as little time and effort as possible. Let's listen to a working mom's story.

Mrs. Chung, a working mom of two children, rents air purifier, clothing care machine, and clothes dryers from an electronics company. The monthly rental fee is about 130,000 won after getting discount from an affiliate credit card company. It might cost less to purchase these appliances considering the rental contract requires him to use them for five years, but she is satisfied with the rental service, because employees from the company visit regularly to sanitize the supply and drainage systems, clean the inside of the machines, and even remove dust from the filter. Mrs. Chung said, "It is great that they take care of these appliances, because I'm not sure how to manage them at all." She continued, "It costs a little money, but I think it's better to save time from housekeeping and spend more time with my children." [7]

This is a good example that demonstrates how most convenium consumers feel. As long as you have the choice of having more comfortable life, consumers are willing to choose that choice, be it a rental service, luxury brand, or subscription service, even though it costs a little more money. In the past, companies were not sure if they should make their products available for rental or subscription to make them more popular. But now, the paradigm of service itself must be changed. Decisions should be made based on consumers' convenience. What is needed most at this time is paying close attention to consumers. If you carefully observe what inconveniences that customers are experiencing, and how they are spending their times, you will see opportunities for new business. Focus on little inconveniences consumers are experiencing and make their life a premium! People say we are in a bad recession, but opportunities still exist.

Elevate yourself

Birth of Self-upgraders

Upgrade yourself! A new type of people who pursues growth rather than success has emerged: Self-Upgrading Humans. They focus on making "today's me better than yesterday's me" rather than on competitions against others. As consumers in the "me-economy" who value themselves the most, they focus on here and now, rather than believing on an unknown future and pursue in "small and sure happiness" in their daily lives. For them, building impressive career tracks to set themselves on the narrow path to success is not meaningful. What matters is daily growth and becoming a better person today than yesterday.

There are three areas these self-upgraders are developing as they envision a full-range of growth in work and life. The first is upgrading one's body through meticulous self-care and exercise, which is hard but made fun by doing it with others. The second is upgrading one's hobbies by exploring new experiences and pleasures. The last is upgrading one's knowledge by extending one's intellectual world by adopting processed knowledge and participating in salons. The ultimate goal of these self-upgraders is to have a hot body, deep hobbies, and hip knowledge.

This self-upgrading trend is partly attributable to social changes in the pursuit of a "work-life balance," triggered by the government policy of a mandatory 52-hour workweek. On a more fundamental level, however, it is a result of the changing paradigm of life and career management in our aging society. With the advent of self-upgraders who desire qualitative changes in their life, an "experience economy" is evolving into a "transformation economy." In a transformation economy, consumers are willing to open their wallet to purchase experiences that help them evolve. Companies need to identify the goals of each consumer and think hard about finding ways to support their growth. The happiness of consumers is moving towards the point of balance between meaningfulness and the fun of self-growth.

Twelve thousand people took the challenge for one goal: Looking at the Sky Once Every Day. Those who took the challenge were required to take a picture of the sky that fills all angles of the camera lens every day for two weeks and upload them on a website. Photos with the sky hidden by a window were not acceptable. Nobody forced them to do it, but they voluntarily paid money to take the challenge and participated in this habit building project. There are diverse goals posted on the Challengers챌린저스, which is a habit building app with a concept of "buying willpower with money." These challenges differ in terms of difficulty levels and areas – getting up at 6:00 am, building six-pack abs in 50 days, transcribing poems, writing reviews after watching movies every week – but they all share one goal: Self-growth.

What would people like to do after they come home from work? In the past, you would have guessed they would kick back and rest in front of the TV, with a beer in hand, trying to rest their tired bodies and minds. However, the evening scene in Korea has changed in the wake of the "work life balance fever" to the point where urban business districts have experienced a drastic change in their sales. Many working people are hurrying somewhere, but they are not headed home. Instead, they are headed to places where they can use those extra hours doing something they enjoy. Some are headed to a cafe with a book, others are headed to the Han River for jogging by the riverside, or to the rental studio exclusively for one-person creators to make a video and upload to their channels. People who have found a quantitative balance between work and life are now trying to find the qualitative change of life.

The original meaning of the word "upgrade" is to improve something a level up, and it is also used to mean using the latest version of computer software to fix errors and improve performance. But now, it has also become an everyday term to mean improving all aspects of life. Therefore, we will call those who are constantly trying to upgrade themselves as "self-upgraders."

The way these self-upgraders invest in themselves is an extension of self-development in building a career. But self-upgraders' commitment to self-development is different from the commitment to building career trajectories. Self-upgraders pursue personal growth over job promotion, dreaming of becoming a better person every day. As the paradigm of self-development changes, the markets that self-upgraders are creating are also upgrading in real time.

A Paradigm Shift from Success to Growth

The self-development program installed by self-upgraders is completely different from "career building" of the past in its goal, intrinsic value and the method of pursuit.

First, "career building" is mostly about building qualifications to put on a resume to find or change a job, and it is mostly carried out by improving scores on foreign language tests or obtaining various licenses and certifications. On the other hand, "upgrading" refers to overall growth in various areas related to a person, such as health, hobbies, knowledge and relationships, beyond the capabilities related to qualifications associated with employment. Therefore, anybody can become a self-upgrader, including job seekers or young salary men and women, as well as full-time moms who wish to be the master of their lives instead of being "somebody's mom," or retired former executives who are preparing a new chapter in their post-retirement life.

If the goal of self-development was becoming "a better me compared to others," the goal of self-upgraders is to become "a better me than yesterday's me." What motivates them is not the anxiety that comes from competing with others, but the anxiety that they might become worse today than they were yesterday. What matters to self-upgraders is not "success," such as entering a famous and prestigious college, or large corporations. When you beat others with your impressive resume and get hired by a prestigious company, it can ensure you good social status for a while, but it does not guarantee a future that is meaningful forever. What self-upgraders pursue is "growth" that will remain as their asset and ensure a good future, instead of the things that are only transitory.

Therefore, the type of growth self-upgraders aim for is not a perfect score on a foreign language test or a top score in a government-administered test. If career building in the past was like filling in an answer sheet for multiple-choice exams, growth for self-upgraders is like writing an essay. The journey to find what you really want, like, and do well to become the hero and heroine of your life can be no less challenging than fierce competition with others. However, while career building is a fight to ensure success in the future at the cost of today, growth for self-upgraders is the process and the goal itself. Therefore, to self-upgraders, "the present time" is like an interesting game that is both fun and meaningful..

Three Ways to Upgrade "Tomorrow's Me"

How and what specifically would the self-upgraders use to upgrade after "growth" became an integral part of their lifestyles? For ordinary people, the three elements of a happy life are health, leisure, and ability, while for the self-upgraders, their consumption for the growth of body, hobbies, and knowledge are direct investments that they can make without sparing anything.

1. Physical Upgrade: Growth is 'Hot'

When you search for a hashtag "Runstagram" on Instagram, you get more than 260,000 results. These posts show flushed faces covered in sweat, and an app screen shot that shows the running distance and heart rate, along with such hashtags as "Woman who exercises" and "Man who exercises," all of which are evidence that they had run hard today as usual. Those are the faces of hot self-upgraders who run every evening to enjoy the "runner's high," which is a feeling similar to walking on cloud nine, a feeling you can get when endorphins are released if you maintain a fast heart rate for more than 30 minutes.

With an increasing population attracted to running, the "running crew" culture – running together with many others – is spreading rapidly among young people. They run in groups with others despite having no clear organizational structure or mandatory condition for participation, because they serve as each other's pacemakers to sustain the race to growth. In fact, it became such a popular activity that the runners who became famous on Instagram are called "runtertainers (run+entertainer)," and now that running itself has emerged as a hot culture, the marathon race, which was considered as an activity only for middle-aged men, has become a national festival enjoyed even by young people.

The latest group exercise program, which is popular among the people in their 20s and 30s, also shows the hot side of the self-upgraders. It has an added fun of meeting other people by mixing men and women in similar gender proportion and fuel their passion for growth by completing the exercise routine together. These programs, founded upon the belief that "anything is possible when in a group," are designed so strictly that participants are sure to achieve growth. One example of the program is about sweating by doing two hours of intensive exercise during weekends, and during weekdays, fulfilling a "home assignment" of exercising at home and diet management. Strict as they may be, they include weekly event-type workouts, and game-like missions to add fun, eventually upgrading exercise to a fun lifestyle enjoyed in a group, instead of a difficult and boring routine. These programs are usually carried out as short-term five week projects. Instead of aiming for a distant future, these programs pick the rules that are possible to follow for a month or two.

The their effort to stay in good shape has brought about changes in the perception of diet. Diet is changing to where people consider their current body condition when comprehensively managing their sleeping time, workout routine, and meal plans and adjust their overall lifestyles to it. This change happening in the upgrading consumption is reflected on the online PT services that are growing popular lately. The difference from the past is that, instead of aiming to lose weight or get pretty, they are more concerned about daily changes necessary to create a healthy lifestyle. To this end, customers record their three meals per day and receive feedback from the coach about what they did well and what they need to improve. It is important to exercise every day, but more than that, they receive one-on-one mental training in this way, because they find it necessary to improve their daily routines through continuous practice. So the question is, why are they putting so much effort into disciplining themselves like athletes who are about to compete in a tournament? Those who have succeeded in keeping their body in good shape claim, "The body does not lie. It gives you back as much as you try." That is the reason the self-upgraders invest so much in their bodies.

2. Hobby Upgrade: Growth is 'Deep'

Another area where self-upgraders enjoy upgrading is their hobbies. They find joy in discovering themselves by enhancing their tastes through hobbies, and experience a sense of achievement through new experiences. The spate of "One Day" classes that are growing popular lately are filled by self-upgraders where they try to enrich themselves with various experiences. Recently, there has been a string of platforms and venues where consumers can find classes on all kinds of hobbies, such as wood carving and silk flower making. The platform Class 101클래스101 is specializing in connecting artists who make novel handcraft works using unique materials and tools with consumers who wish to create their own special artwork. In addition, users of the platform can purchase all the materials that they need and gain the basic knowledge necessary to create a piece of artwork, such as how to use a certain tool, so that they can continuously enjoy the hobby.

Today, more people find "having a good rest" on a vacation or during a hocance (hotel + vacation) not sufficiently satisfying. While the conventional getaway or vacation in a hotel was all about taking a rest and enjoying entertainment, the keyword "learning" has been added for self-upgrading vacationers. Some of the popular vacation packages for travelers who are looking for diverse learning experiences include Florist Tour where people can take a three-day class at a famous flower arrangement shop in Europe; China Business Learning Tour where they can learn the latest business trends in Beijing and Shanghai; and Photo-shooting in Canada where they can learn photography from professional photographers. Vacationing in a hotel is the same. There are hotels that promise a special experience to vacationers while enjoying the luxury and private atmosphere of a hotel, such as a tea ceremony class they can take in a small group or a French cooking class, all of which are taught by invited professionals in their respective areas.

When consumers dig deep into a certain subject or product until they discover the gemstone that they are looking for, we call this behavior "digging consumption." If somebody told you, "I took a short trip to Japan to have sushi," you would have thought it was a joke from a comedy program on TV, but now, it doesn't strike anyone as odd because "digging consumers" wish to have the perfect experience. For the digging consumers who dig into sushi, their digging ends only when they visit Japan, the home of sushi, go the sushi restaurant rated number one on Tabelog (restaurant search app in Japan), taste their sushi, and take photos to upload on their social media to prove that they've been there and experienced it. There is also a soba version, in which the digging consumers not only visit Japan to taste local soba dishes, they also bring home materials and cooking tools so that they can personally make noodles and cook soba from scratch at home. The digging consumers in the cultural sector are also demonstrating commitment comparable to professionals in their areas of interest. In the past, a movie mania meant somebody who watches movies from all genres, but today, a digging movie fan digs up only one specific genre of movies. There are even those who dig for just one specific movie numerous times. Called "N times watching," this latest trend is about watching the same movie over and over to analyze the narrative structure, mise-en-scéne, and whatever else they want to analyze to discover metaphors and symbols that other people may have missed. According to CGV Research Center, there was a digging movie fan who watched the movie, the *Handmaiden*, 111 times.[1]

3. Knowledge Upgrade: Growth is 'Hip'

Peter Drucker has pointed out that the current information society will be followed by the knowledge society. In knowledge society, knowledge is a means of production, and knowledge workers who know how to utilize their knowledge become the new capitalists.

We are actually already living in knowledge society. People enjoy watching a TV program where famous writers, professors and experts dine together and converse on a variety of topics. Career men and women are willing to pay expensive membership fees to join book clubs to enjoy intellectual conversations and experience healing through intellectual discourse.

All these cases demonstrate that the knowledge-devouring society is here. Knowledge-seeking consumers are the hipsters in the knowledge society because they are committed to becoming trendy intellectuals by keeping pace with social change and seeking developments in the most recent knowledge. They are willing to subscribe and pay for various knowledge content items because they do not want to miss any of it.

The e-book subscription service market that has been growing lately is attracting the self-upgrading consumers who are always hungry for knowledge. Millie's Study밀리의서재, a website that spearheaded e-book subscription service in Korea, recorded 700,000 subscribers in the two years after its launch, with each subscriber reading an average of eight books per month.[2]

These numbers are not just significant as indicators of how many people read how many books. Korea's largest e-book distributor Ridi Books리디북스 reported that visitors stayed at the website for 1 hour, 12 minutes and 59 seconds on average in January 2019, which is a 77.4 percent increase from the previous year when it was 41 minutes and nine seconds. This number is higher than the amount of time people spent on YouTube (1 hour, 26 minutes, two seconds), which recently became the leading pastime for Koreans, and even Instagram (24 minutes 57 seconds).[3]

Now that the amount of data produced around the world in one day is nearly 650 billion times the volume of a *Harry Potter* book[4], the self-upgrading consumers who don't want to fall behind in a knowledge society try to acquire a vast amount of knowledge faster and easier. Watching book review videos is one of their knowledge acquiring activities. On YouTube, there are many prolific Booktubers who review books and even offer many insights on the topic to think about. There are many other knowledge subscription services for other types of information as well, including: Newneek뉴닉 that compiles various news reports and sends them to over 60,000 subscribers in the form of a newsletter that appeals to millennials; Uppity어피티 that is a kind of economic newsletter popular among young people early in their career track; and D-dock디독 that compiles only design-related articles from overseas for subscribers.

The self-upgrading consumers are not hesitant to spend money for quality information, either. One example is Publy 퍼블리, which claims to be "a content platform for working people," and provides subscribers with industry trends and insights from people who are currently working in various industries. The web service showed a promising future for knowledge-providing paid service business by recording over 20,000 cumulative subscribers who are willing to pay about 20,000 won per month for the service.

When it comes to knowledge-related growth, self-upgraders are not satisfied with just being receivers. Groups where they can achieve a secondary expansion of knowledge by sharing their insights with others are growing popular. The startup Trevari트레바리 has grown into a major community service with over 5,600 members in 344 book clubs in just four years. This service is considered the most typical example of the modern day salon patronized by self-upgraders. Each book club has about 20 members and each season in which the book club runs consists of four monthly meetings where members read and discuss books on a certain theme of their choice. The theme could be crime stories, ancient philosophy, entrepreneurship, or Murakami Haruki's work. Members can attend a meeting only when they have read the book and submitted a book review. It costs money to join the book club and it takes time and effort to write a book review each month, but people choose to attend these meetings because they enjoy sharing deep thoughts about certain subjects and growing through intellectual exchanges with each other.

Background to the Rise of the Self-upgraders

Growth Matters More Than Success

The emergence of self-upgraders who proactively explore their lives begins with a shift in perspective on what success means. Success can be defined in many ways, but traditionally, success meant winning a social title that guarantees wealth and honor by successfully competing with others. However, self-upgraders are the pioneers of the "me-me-land" who care about their own happiness rather than being compared to or having to compete with others. The trend of placing importance on one's self began several years ago. The "self-esteem" trend identified in *Trend Korea 2018* discussed people who sought centeredness in the self in an unstable society, and the "me-me land" trend in *Trend Korea 2019* pointed out the beginning of the "meconomy", or the "economy for my own self", supported by those who broke free from the judging eyes of others and determined that they would live according to their own beliefs about life.

In addition, the changed frame of happiness has motivated people to aim for growth as their goal in life. The concept of happiness itself has changed, and now, people believe the present matters more than the future, daily life matters more than non-daily life, and frequency matters more than intensity. The latest growth trends fit this frame of happiness well. People are moving forward not for the glory of tomorrow, but for an "I who is better tomorrow than today," and for a tangible accomplishment rather than a grand vision. People can feel the thrilling sense of achievement from developing even a small habit instead of from accomplishing an impressive feat.

Growth is both a present-oriented pleasure and a realistic way to prepare for the future. Life is too long to live only for present pleasure. Now that life expectancy is hovering up to 100 years, people today have only a "half-lifelong job" instead of a "lifelong job" even if they are guaranteed to work until they hit 60 before retiring. Even though today's growth does not guarantee a comfortable tomorrow, there is no question that nothing will be changed tomorrow if nothing is done today. Those who have found a balance between work and personal life need a structural realignment of their perspective on life. It is undeniable that they have to seek growth in the three mainstay factors of life: health, hobbies and abilities.

Many Roads Lead to Growth

The second reason for self-upgraders to pursue changes and growth in their own way has a lot to do with the disintegration of standardized phases of the life cycle.

Just as a story unfolds in the order of introduction, development, turn, and conclusion, so has the life cycle of man. The stereotyped phases of a life cycle as a family member used to be marriage, child birth, raising children, and the independence of children, while the life cycle as a working man used to be hired, repetition of a job assignment, promotion, repetition of a job assignment, and retirement. Living these cycles of life and work, people did not worry too much about their personal growth. But now that marriage and childbirth have become a matter of personal choice, and a growing number of people are managing their own career portfolios instead of staying at one job forever, having their own story plot became necessary.

The emergence of temporary communities such as "Crews" and "Salons" can be explained in the same context. People's identity is no longer solely linked to family, school, work or local communities. In a society where collectivity has been dismantled and completely reorganized to become individual-oriented, each individual's identity is segmented into parts depending on each individuals' unique circumstances and preferences. Now, people are less reluctant to temporarily share their ride with those who are headed in the same direction, as we can see in the running crew, taste community, and book salon. They feel a sense of belonging in terms of values and goals, instead of in terms of people.

The era of YouTube where "everybody is the main character" has also attributed to the rise of self-upgraders and has facilitated them in taking more proactive actions in pursuit of their growth. In the last few years, it has become commonplace to observe ordinary people, not just famous celebrities, standing in front of an audience and telling stories about their growth. With the widely spreading media culture centered on one person, successful creators also share their stories about how they became successful, and what they have tried, on their channels. The existence of relatable role models instead of superstar role models who seem to be out of most people's reach has become a powerful motivation for growth.

In a transformation economy, consumers
are willing to open their wallet to purchase
experiences that help them evolve. Companies
need to identify the goals of each consumer and
think hard about finding ways to support their
growth.

Implications

What changes will the rise of these self-upgraders who pursue daily betterment bring to the market? Primarily, the growth of self-development related industries is expected. Services designed to offer foreign language or job-related training and other learning services are expected to grow. In particular, these services should be provided to match individual goals and lifestyles. Like the online PT service that was addressed earlier, small groups are meticulously customized for individuals to manage their life as a whole, or where dynamic interaction with each other is expected to be their preferred choice. That is the reason large lecture-type educational services are declining while one-on-one tutoring-type systems are growing through online talent exchange platforms.

In addition, efforts should be focused on designing experiences that can make growth efforts enjoyable for the self-upgraders who pursue growth not at the cost of the present but as a pleasing lifestyle. A few good examples are the gamification that is similar to a level system and game mission that many service providers have adopted already. System design that promises sure growth is also attractive.

Self-upgraders envision an all-around improvement in the quality of their life. People will open their wallets to anything that can cause positive ripple effects on the way they work and live. We are now in the "change economy" or the "transformation economy." In 1999, Pine and Gilmore proposed the concept of the "experience economy." Under the experience economy, which comes after the commodity economy and the service economy, positive experience gained from products and services becomes value worth paying for. Furthermore, Pine and Gilmore also mentioned the "change economy" as the next step following the experience economy. In the change economy, the joy of experiencing products and services is not limited to the moment of consumption, and it extends to create values that can induce positive changes in the lives of consumers. In other words, if companies in the experience economy offered special experiences to consumers and made them fall in love with their brands, in the change economy, consumers should be encouraged to blend into their brands and let the brands breathe in their lives.

In fact, the transition to the change economy has already begun. The pioneering brands that practice change economy include Lululemon and Nike. In the case of Lululemon, the company motivates customers to personally practice the "sweat life" which the company envisions, instead of directly encouraging consumers to buy their products. Lululemon, a company that started as a local community base and still offers various free yoga and wellness classes at its stores, sponsored the Wanderlust Festival, the first worldwide wellness festival held in Korea in August 2019, to motivate consumers to experience the sweat life as a festival. In the case of Nike, it is not an overstatement to say that Nike has been spearheading the running culture. The "Nike Run Club (NRC)" run by Nike has now become a must-have app for runners. Nike has been supporting running life by holding regular running events and donating limited edition shoes that it has developed in collaboration with running crews.

If businesses wish to support the evolution of consumers in the transformation economy, they first have to understand the evolution that consumers want. Brand strategy specialist Jasmine Bina stated that in order to understand the consumers who always dream of changes, businesses have to understand not only "being" but also "becoming."[5] Consumers no longer remain static, such as a man, thirty-something, or office worker. They are in a state of "becoming" through changes that repeatedly happen every day, such as "becoming a body with 15 percent less body fat," "becoming an owner of a small craft shop," or "becoming the founder of a startup in five years." If you have one piece of customer data now, that is just a snapshot of the change process. To ensure that what you provide to your customers has the value of change, you must know what changes your consumers want, and what they value.. And you have to think hard to find out how you can blend your brand into their journey.

There are two pillars of happiness: pleasure and a sense of

purpose. A sense of purpose implies a sense of achievement, meaningfulness, and reward. In order to achieve maximum happiness that will not evaporate over time, the activities that fill our lives need to strike a proper balance between pleasure and a sense of purpose. Growth that self-upgraders are after is an activity that contributes to both pleasure and a sense of purpose. If our discourses on happiness had their focus only on immediate pleasure until now, the rise of self-upgraders signifies that the weight of happiness is slowly moving towards the sense of purpose. Now, the balance between pleasure and meaningfulness is becoming more important.

Notes

Me and Myselves: Multi-persona

1 소영(2016), "다중정체성을 통한 트랜스 아이덴티티의 확장: 영화 〈홀리 모터스〉를 중심으로", 〈외국문학연구〉, 64, 2016, 73~92P.

2 "우리는 Z 세대이다", 〈오토모티브리포트〉, 2018.05.31.

3 "나를 위한 비밀 계정 필수"… SNS 계정 늘리는 2030", 〈이데일리〉, 2019.06.23.

4 "'열린 광장'에서 '안락한 거실'로", 〈중앙시사매거진〉, 2019.04.08.

5 *Je Selfie Donc Je suis, Elsa Godart* 2016, Éditions Albin Michel.

6 "SNS 속 나는 거리에서 또 다른 나를 '창발'한다", 〈경향신문〉, 2019.09.10.

7 이졸데 카림, 『나와 타자들』 이승희 옮김, 민음사, 2019.

8 "노브랜드버거 10만개 팔렸다는데… 햄버거에 꽂힌 정용진, 왜", 〈중앙일보〉, 2019.10.09.

9 "'GRWM'이 뭐지?… 요즘 새롭게 뜨는 유튜브 트렌드 5", 〈한경비즈니스〉, 2019.06.25.

10 "소셜미디어와 익명성-자유에 대한 은근한 열망", 서기슬 브런치 (brunch.co.kr/@itandesire/4), 2019.07.06.

Immediate Satisfaction : 'Last Fit Economy'

1 "한샘·현대리바트, 배송전쟁 '후끈'", 〈건설경제신문〉, 2019.08.07.

2 "'동네 사람만 와라' 이랬더니 대박 터진 AI 벼룩시장", 〈중앙일보〉, 2019.09.22.

3 "'마지막 1마일을 잡아라'… 완성차업계 '전동킥보드' 大戰", 〈매일경제〉, 2019.10.03.

4 "사업 다각화·특화 상품으로 돌파구 찾는 여행업계", 〈뉴스토마토〉, 2019.08.23.

Goodness and Fairness : Fair Player

1 "줄 서기의 심리학: 내가 더 기다리는 한이 있어도 새치기는 못 봐줘", 〈ㅍㅍㅅㅅ〉, 2018.10.12.

2 "퍼시스, 사무실이 카페처럼… 소통 이끄는 '플레이웍스' 소파", 〈서울경제〉, 2019.09.25.

3 Chung, I., & Park, H., "Educational expansion and trends in intergenerational social mobility among Korean men", *Social Science Research*, 83, 2019.

4 武器になる哲学 人生を生き抜くための哲学・思想のキーコンセプト50, Yamaguchi Shu, 2018, Kadokawa

Here and Now: the 'Streaming Life'

1 "힙스터의 뉴욕 아파트 월세는 얼마", 신세계 빌리브 웹진(villiv.co.kr/space/2488).

2 "구독경제 Subscription Economy", 〈매일경제〉, 2019.03.27.

3 "판 커지는 자동차 구독 시장-트렌드는 맞는데… 비싼 월정액 부담되네", 〈매경이코노미〉, 2019.07.15.

4 "우버콥터료 23만원… '하늘택시' 시대 성큼", 〈문화일보〉, 2019.07.10.

5 "앱으로 예약하면 우버 잠수함이 '내 앞에'… 가격은 얼마?", 〈머니투데이〉, 2019.05.28.

6 "'구독경제', 소유와 공유를 뛰어넘다", 〈메가경제〉, 2019.04.28.

7 "판 커지는 자동차 구독 시장-트렌드는 맞는데… 비싼 월정액 부담되네", 〈매경이

코노미〉, 2019.07.15.

8   "신문부터 요트까지… 커지는 '구독경제' 시장", 〈노컷뉴스〉, 2019.04.14.

9   "영화·음악·침대·자동차까지… 이젠 갖지 않고 '구독'", 〈중앙SUNDAY〉,
2019.04.20.

Technology of Hyper-personalization

1   "5 Brands Taking Personalized Marketing To The Next Level", *Forbes*,
2018.12.28.

2   *GAFA×BATH 米中メガテックの競争戦略*, Tanaka Michiaki, 2019,
Nikkeibook

3   "You Now Have a Shorter Attention Span Than a Goldfish", *TIME*,
2015.05.14.

4   애덤 알터, 『멈추지 못하는 사람들』 홍지수 옮김, 부키, 2019.

5   *Irresistible: The Rise of Addictive Technology and the Business of Keeping Us Hooked*,
Adam Alter, 2017, Penguin Press

6   "삼성도 AI 스피커 시장 참전… '갤럭시 홈 미니' 출시 임박", 〈아시아경제〉,
2019.09.11.

7   "초개인화 - 클릭을 넘어, 발자국을 짚어내는 마케팅의 진화(2)", 〈동아일보〉,
2019.07.09.

8   프랭클린 포어, 『생각을 빼앗긴 세계』 박상현·이승연 옮김, 반비, 2019.

You're with Us, 'Fansumer'

1   "규제 푼 크라우드 펀딩, 투자자 늘고 펀딩규모도 커져", 〈뉴스토마토〉,
2019.07.08.

2   "'카톡'으로 배우 조종… 영화 결말도 직접 고른다", 〈이데일리〉, 2019.08.13.

3   "'해외 팬클럽과 왜 차별하나요'… 성난 팬덤, 일부는 '탈덕'까지", 〈동아일보〉,
2019.07.27.

Make or Break, Specialize or Die

1 "스포츠용품 시장 뒤집은 여자들", 〈조선일보〉, 2019.09.25.

2 통계청, 〈2017년 인구주택총조사〉, 2018.08.27.

3 "빕스 앤 비어바이트, 세계·수제맥주 '팔찌만 대면 콸콸'", 〈아주경제〉, 2019.03.29.

Iridescent OPAL: the New 5060 Generation

1 미래에셋은퇴연구소, "5가지 키워드로 본 5060세대의 가족과 삶", 〈2018 미래에셋 은퇴라이프트렌드 조사보고서〉, 2018.05.04.

2 "유튜브 보고… 모바일 쇼핑하고… 5070 우리가 알던 '폰맹'이 아닙니다", 〈한국경제〉, 2019.05.16.

3 "TV리모컨 놓고 유튜브 트는 5060", 〈동아일보〉, 2019.05.15.

4 "'1,500명 전문가 매칭' 탤런트뱅크, 中企문제 해결사로 각광", 〈매일경제〉, 2019.08.11.

5 "여행을 꿈꾸는 대한민국 시니어들", 익스피디아 브런치(brunch.co.kr/@expediakr/111), 2016.11.01.

6 "애비야~'인싸'라 불러다오", 〈이데일리〉, 2019.05.03.

7 "모두를 위한 '간편' 결제를 찾아서", 〈블로터〉, 2019.09.09.

8 "'내 나이가 어때서'… '에이지리스 쇼핑' 즐기는 4060 '꽃중년'", 〈이데일리〉, 2018.08.13.

9 *Longevity Economy* by Joseph F. Coughlin, Public Affairs, 2017.

Convenience as a Premium

1 "어릴 적 엄마가 들려주던 동화처럼 '귀로 읽는 책'… 디지털시대 新독서법", 〈영남일보〉, 2019.06.27.

2 "'아이돌보미 플랫폼' 맘시터, 신규투자 30억 원 유지", 〈서울경제〉, 2019.05.17.

3 "분수대 → 워터파크 → 인피니티 풀… 아파트 커뮤니티시설 경쟁", 〈조선비즈〉, 2019.07.08.

4 "효율성 최강의 다이어트 '크라이오 +EMS'", 〈헤럴드경제〉, 2019.06.04.

5 Granovetter, S. M., "The Strength of Weak Ties", *American Journal of*

Sociology, 78(6), 1973.

6 ""마음껏 게으르게 사세요~"", 〈동아일보〉, 2019.06.08.

Elevate Yourself : Birth of Self-upgraders

1 "영화보기 본질 바꾼 'N차 관람' 현상", 〈중앙SUNDAY〉, 2018.12.22.

2 "100억… 300억… 투자 몰리는 독서 스타트업", 〈조선일보〉, 2019.04.09.

3 "月정액 전자책' 돌풍", 〈한국경제〉, 2019.03.24.

4 "전 세계서 하루 생산되는 데이터, 해리포터 책 6,500억 권 분량… '최고데이터책임자(CDO)' 속속 신설하는 기업들", 〈WEEKLY BIZ〉, 2018.10.05.

5 "In the Transformational Economy, 'Being' and 'Becoming' Have Started To Merge", medium.com/@TripleJas/in-the-transformational-economy-being-becoming-have-started-to-merge-d821501bf28), 2018.03.13.